THE LETTER

JANIE JACKS

THE ROADRUNNER PRESS
OKLAHOMA CITY, OKLAHOMA

The RoadRunner Press
Oklahoma City, Oklahoma
www.TheRoadRunnerPress.com

This is a work of fiction. While the literary perceptions and insights are based on experience, all names, characters, places, and incidents are either products of the author's imagination or are used fictitiously.

First edition published October 2023.
Printed in the USA.

For group and book club sales, please contact your favorite bookstore, online retailer, or wholesaler—or email info@theroadrunnerpress.com.

Library of Congress Control Number: 2023938283

Publisher's Cataloging-in-Publication
(Provided by Cassidy Cataloguing Services, Inc.)
Names: Jacks, Janie, author.
Title: The letter / Janie Jacks.
Description: First edition. | Oklahoma City, Oklahoma : The RoadRunner Press, 2023.
Identifiers: ISBN: 978-1937054939 (hardcover) | 978-1950871131 (trade paper) |
        978-1950871223 (ebook/epub) | LCCN: 2023938283
Subjects: LCSH: Families of military personnel--United States--Fiction. | Letters--Fiction.
        | Vietnam War, 1961-1975--Fiction. | Mothers and daughters--Fiction. | Curios-
        ity--Fiction. | LCGFT: Historical fiction. | Domestic fiction. | BISAC: FAMILY
        & RELATIONSHIPS / Military Families. | FICTION / Women. | FICTION
        / War & Military.
Classification: LCC: PS3610.A3447 L48 2023 | DDC: 813/.6--dc23

10 9 8 7 6 5 4 3 2 1

*To my children and every other child who sent
a parent to the Vietnam War*

CHAPTER 1

Pryor, Oklahoma
August 2010

THE JOURNAL WAS TUCKED under some old gym shorts in the bottom drawer of the walnut dresser in my childhood bedroom—a room that for years had served as a haven for returning siblings and the occasional houseguest.

Nothing much about the room had changed since it had been my personal teen domain, from the pink-striped wallpaper and cherub lamps to the old gold-framed mirror into which I had gazed for many an hour primping and wishing and wondering what my future would bring.

I had spent the morning rummaging through drawers and closets full of high-school junk, trying to decide what to keep from those teenage days and what to trash. Mama had summoned her children home to Pryor, Oklahoma, declaring that whatever remained from our childhood after month's end would be thrown out. She had been making the same threat for years. This time, we all knew she was serious.

So Pat, Scott, and I had come home.

Getting the three of us together in one place was a rare occurrence anymore, and Mama braced all of us up at attention immediately upon our arrival, which was not. "I'm through storing your stuff," she said, waving her arms for emphasis. "My garage looks like a junk shed. The only way I could think of to get you to come and get your things was to threaten to move. So I'm threatening—to move. Everything has to go. I'm tired of cleaning around all of your high-school leftovers."

Her threat sounded sincere, but who could know if Mama meant it or not. She had, however, never threatened to move before.

"You're all married and gone, and I'm ready for something more manageable," she said. "Smaller, but with a big vegetable garden in the backyard. I want less inside and more outside."

She raised her arms again for emphasis, then dropped them and took a breath. "I don't want to dust anymore. So get your stuff out; take some of mine. Take whatever you want. Because if you don't empty the rest of those boxes in the garage and the shed, whatever is in them is going to the Methodist church rummage sale or to the dump. I stored most of those boxes because you three kept telling me not to throw any of them away." She gave each of us a stern look. "You know what I am saying is true. So let's do this. Now!"

We lined up in a row military fashion—as we had been raised— with my older sister Pat leading the way to the garage.

Once there, Mama checked to be sure she had our attention before pointing to the dusty shelves closest to the ceiling. "The boxes on the top two shelves haven't been opened since we moved here more than thirty-five years ago. I'll take responsibility for those. I know what's in them. I just haven't gotten around to . . . I kept meaning to . . . go through them, throw some of it away, but . . . anyway, Scott, you and I can do those together later."

Her voice trailed off as she looked up at all the unopened boxes high on the top shelf neatly labeled: "Uniforms. Flight logs. Medals and citations." She turned and looked at us and said, "I mean it. I'll do that top row of boxes, but the rest is up to you three. If you don't get your things out of here, they're gone. I suggest you start by getting rid of all your school stuff."

We didn't bother to protest.

"Okay," Scott replied, "I'll get a ladder and move those boxes off the top shelf, Mama. I'll help you go through those this weekend. I promise."

Dust wafted from above, settling on us like mist as Scott handed the boxes down one by one to Pat and me. Mama watched our progress, occasionally brushing dust clouds away from her face. "Scott, you promise you'll be back to help me go through those other ones?"

"Cross my heart. Ten o'clock Saturday morning. If you'll fix me breakfast, I'll come earlier."

"Done. Pancakes, eggs, and bacon."

"Okay. Make it eight-thirty, then."

"Promise?"

"Yep. Promise."

Mama wagged her finger at each of us, repeating her order one last time. "Out! Every football program. Every yearbook. Every dried prom corsage. Every single thing—out!"

I had come home for a week as requested to do my part—to dig through those old corsages from forgotten proms, ribbons from gymnastic meets, cheerleading pom-poms, and the rest of the odds and ends that accumulate over the first eighteen years of a girl's life only to be forgotten after high-school graduation.

In the middle of the mess in my bedroom, I found my old journal, the one I had written before we made the move from South Carolina to Oklahoma. Before we were uprooted and our lives were torn apart.

That wonderful *before.*

Back in the 1960s, I had kept the journal off and on for a few years. Now that seemed a million years ago—back when I was a little girl learning to record the events that occurred in my perfectly encapsulated world. As journals go, it was never much. The first entry read:

Five crabs and one gray snail today.

Followed by the unremarkable question:

Why isn't my mother curious? It's driving me crazy!

Two sentences that perfectly summed up the important details of my life at the time, as seen through the eyes of a seven-year-old. Two

3

short entries from a time when I was unaware that life could hold pain or loss. Two short entries that dated back to a time when our lives were full of joy. Before the day the letter came and everything changed, never to be the same again. They say you can't go home again, but in my dreams, sometimes I go there, drifting through time in my mind.

Back to Beaufort.

CHAPTER 2

SCOOTER AND I HAD SPENT the morning on the beach
catching crabs, sand and sea all around us, the sun toasting our
salt-encrusted arms and legs to a warm golden brown.

We tied strings around our best bait, a chicken neck, and threw it
into the softly rippling tidal basin, slowly dragging the baited line back
through the water and onto the sand. The googly-eyed creatures that
hid in the reeds offshore spotted and locked onto the bloody temptation, hanging onto the chicken neck even as my brother and I scooped
the crabs up and into our buckets.

"Hey, Scooter! I caught the biggest crab ever!" I yelled. "Look at
those pinchers!"

My brother's name was actually Scott, but nobody ever called him
that except Mom. Scooter fit him much better. My brother came running to see what monster crab I had caught. He leaned down to where I
was squatting beside my bucket and peered inside, gave the crab a good
examination and then poked it a couple of times with a stick.

"It's a big 'en, Beebe," he whispered. "A really, really big 'en." Then
with the mischief for which he was notorious, Scooter stood, dumped
his bucket of crabs on my head, and took off running down the beach

as fast as he could go, squealing at the top of his voice, "You can't catch me! Nope, you can't! I's got the fastest feets in the world!"

He knew what would happen next. It was the part he liked best. With a crab in each hand, I jumped up and followed him, chasing Scooter through the sand until I managed to grab his ankle and tackle him. We tumbled over each other, covered in sand, gasping for breath.

"Hep me, some-bod-ee! Hep me!" Scooter yelled. "Crab Girl's a-gonna kill me. Hep!"

Scooter loved to make noise and he dearly loved to run. Yelling and running full speed were how he lived life. He was two years younger than I was but almost my size. People said we looked like bookends. And because he was almost as tall as me, everyone thought he was older than he looked.

Until he spoke.

Then you knew he was just a little boy.

Tanned, with brown eyes and long legs, Scooter had hair bleached white from the sun. We looked alike, but I envied his long legs; my little brother was lanky and built like a gazelle. When he ran, he seemed to float above the ground, and when he jumped, with his arms out wide, you were sure the laws of gravity were about to be repealed, and he was going to fly. Watching him run was pure joy. Perfection in motion. Barefoot, in cutoffs and a sleeveless T-shirt—he looked like a miniature beach bum, a striking, picture-book, perfectly formed, beautiful boy.

He was my best friend.

Scooter was better at catching crabs than I was. He could cast bait and make it land in the water exactly where he wanted it to go. He loved to throw things. Give him a ball, and he could throw it to land on target, so throwing a chicken neck required only a few minor adjustments for its shape. The hardest part of crabbing for Scooter was being quiet as we dragged the crabs in. I was better at the quiet part. Scooter was better at casting a line.

The day would come when I could no longer catch him, but that summer, I was still bigger and faster and stronger than my little brother. I would tackle him and tickle him until he gave up, and then we would start the game all over again, throwing chicken necks out into the water, dragging crabs back to shore on our strings. Filling our buckets with treasure until it was time to go home. Perfect fun.

The endless days of summer stretched out before us, and time stood still. It was a magical time, and my little brother and I were part of the magic.

CHAPTER 3

WE LIVED IN LAUREL BAY MILITARY HOUSING on the water, just outside Beaufort, South Carolina, halfway between Savannah and Charleston. Right smack-dab in the middle of heaven. When the tide was in, water from the backwater bay lapped up to the end of our street, and twice each day, the tide went out, sucking debris with it, cleaning the sand, and leaving little shells and other treasure behind.

Our house was a stone's throw from the beach. Ancient live oaks growing in twisted, swaying columns along our street marched in a line down to the water and spread away from the street and houses into dark, musty woods. Live oaks overshadowed our world. Gnarled and wrinkled like the faces of old men covered with gray, dripping beards of Spanish moss, their hurricane-deformed limbs stretched long arms over shaded, leaf-cluttered paths that beckoned us down to the teeming tidal pools.

At night, the soft ocean winds whispered through the trees, blowing the draping tendrils of Spanish moss back and forth in the cool damp night air, swaying like dancing ghosts in the haunted woods of the deep, dark South. The silence of the night would descend like a heavy blanket, muffling the sounds of frogs, owls, and the creeping things that rustled through the damp leaves that carpeted the ground.

Summer mornings were all alike. Wake up. Eat Cocoa Puffs. Throw on our shorts, sandals, and baseball caps. Head for the beach to catch crabs, noodle for little backwater creatures, or pick up shells. Some days, we built sandcastles. Crabs became our captive dragons, locked up in carefully crafted walls ready to fend off imaginary pirates lurking offshore. Sea-grass swords were brandished when pirates approached, and battles raged until the pirates were defeated. We were always the heroic victors of our battles. Eventually, however, the castle walls would fall to the frothy foam of the incoming tide, and we would release our crab-dragons, dust the sand off our legs, and head home for a peanut-butter-and-jelly sandwich with a cold glass of milk.

After lunch, we were off again to the cool of the woods to escape the rising afternoon heat. We would play amid the towering old oaks where it was shady and where the damp, humid climate bred all manner of creepy, crawly forest creatures that slinked, slid, and hid beneath leaf and rock, waiting to be found, caught, teased with a twig, and then released to carry on their way. Afternoons were for climbing trees, looking for snakes, and catching frogs—or maybe playing tag, hide-and-seek, or war with the neighborhood kids.

Evenings, we gathered with our friends and chased lightning bugs, catching and sticking them in Mason jars to light up the night or pasting their glowing tails on our faces, while we ran after each other in the dark. It was all perfectly frightening. The darkness and our glowing bug-tail faces added an eerie backdrop to a spooky, forbidding, deep southern nighttime. Scary without any real danger. The best kind of scary.

Eventually somebody's parent would call, "Come on in—it's time to get ready for bed," and we would all trudge home, take a bath, and climb into our beds dead tired. We fell asleep instantly, dreaming through the night of doing the same thing we had done that day all over again the next day. Every day. Our summer routine never paled. We slept well, knowing another day of sun, tide, sea life, critters, and friends awaited us in the morning.

We could count on that.

I was seven years old that summer of 1966, and my world was perfect. Warm, sunshiny days stretched out like a soft carpet before me, unending and wonderful—until that June morning when Scooter and I returned home for lunch, the day I caught my biggest crab ever and found the unopened letter on the table.

CHAPTER 4

THE TABLE WHERE I FIRST SAW the letter was an old one—in years, not for our family. Cherrywood, with spooled gatelegs and two side leaves that hung almost to the carpet. The wood smelled of lemon oil and Johnson's wax, both applied for who knows how many years, with a generous amount of grease. The elbow kind.

In the evenings, it was my job to pull the table leaves up, swivel out the gatelegs, and set out our pink china plates, cloth napkins, and silver for supper. We rarely used paper napkins; my father liked linen on the table for meals when he was home.

"People are having a hard time making ends meet," he would say. "They're selling off all their grandmas' wedding linens in yard sales, and your mama keeps buying them, so we might as well put them on our table and enjoy them."

"One more thing to wash and iron," Mama would say.

"Then how come you buy them?" Daddy would ask.

"Just to make you happy, Ken," Mama would say. She would be grinning by then. "Anyway, all that handwork, it's a shame to let it go to waste. Someone's grandmother did all that needlework, and then nobody ever used it. That grandma put away what she'd created in a hope chest for fifty, sixty years, waiting for a special occasion that never came. That's why those beautiful embroidered napkins ended up in a yard sale for me to find and buy."

"And for me to wipe the gravy off my chin," Daddy would add.

Mama had bought the old table with a war bond she had purchased while still a little girl, during World War II. She had saved her dimes to buy the bond to support the war. Everybody was doing the same back then because the government was broke and needed to borrow money from its citizens to build tanks and airplanes to fight the Nazis. Two decades later, that twenty-five-dollar bond was the grand sum total of our family's savings.

The day Mama bought the table, Daddy was in Okinawa, eating three meals a day with linen napkins on linen tablecloths in the officers' club. Me, Mama, and Pat were in Pryor, Oklahoma, living month to month on his Marine Corps check, one that didn't cover fol-de-rol like cherry gateleg tables, linen napkins, and such. The check barely covered the car payment and one tank of gasoline, which we usually burned up the first week of every month looking for stuff we couldn't buy because we didn't have any money left. Mama would throw the double stroller in the car, and off we would go. Driving and looking. Those drives were our only entertainment. Three girls—me, Mama, and Pat—waiting out the year for my daddy to come home.

One afternoon, while wandering through a junk store, Mama came to a sudden halt. "Well, look at that!" she said. "A cherry table with turned spool legs!" She walked around the table a couple of times, pulled the leaves out, rotated one of the gatelegs, then stood appraising it with her hands on her hips. "People need a table to eat on, and we girls don't have one."

We also didn't have a house or a dining room. We were living with my grandparents. Yet to hear my mother tell the way-you-make-big-decisions story, every important decision Mama's family had ever made was around their dining table.

"It's important to have a place to gather in the evenings and to eat supper. And talk. We don't have one. A drop leaf would be perfect since it wouldn't take up much space. If we have a dining room, I'll put it there. And if we don't, I'll put it next to the sofa and use it as an end table and put a lamp on top. When I get a sofa. And a lamp." I could tell Mama had convinced herself we had to have the table if we were ever going to be a proper family; the old war bond made it possible.

Thirteen months later, when my father returned from Japan, he took one look at the table and said, "Sweetheart, exactly how were you planning to get that thing from Oklahoma to Virginia? You, me, two girls, and a table—in a pink compact sedan?" Over the years, Daddy told this story so often, I knew all the lines by heart. The table story was one of his favorite stories he liked to tell about the things Mama did that were, as he liked to say, "*Iffy. . . . If this, if that.*"

The day Daddy saw the table for the first time, he looked at it, looked at Mama, and grinned, "You want it on top of the car. You want us to drive from Oklahoma to my new assignment in Virginia with that table turned upside down on top of a pink Rambler. Huh? On top of the car? Bad enough you traded my car in on a Rambler. But pink?" Daddy shook his head. "No way I can drive a pink car to work, much less drive to Virginia with a table on top of it." We kids knew he wasn't really mad at Mama because he couldn't keep from smiling.

"Well, I thought the car was pretty," Mama said. "Your car was ruined, and besides, it was old. This car is new, and the payments are lower. I got a good deal and I like pink."

The car that Daddy had left behind for us to drive while he was overseas had been previously caught in an Oklahoma sideways-blow-through-every-nook-and-cranny rainstorm. The kind of thunderstorm for which Oklahoma is well known. When Mama wrote and told him about the damage to the family car, he told her to trade the car in. I doubt the color ever came up.

"A captain in the U. S. Marine Corps driving to work in a pink car. I'll never live it down," he said. "Did you ever wonder why it was so cheap? Do you think it might have been the color?" No longer able to keep a straight face, he was chuckling now.

And that's how we went to Quantico, Virginia—like Okies in *The Grapes of Wrath*. Except we headed east instead of west with a gateleg table (not a mattress) lashed to the roof of the car. Spool legs sticking straight up toward the sky with ropes running through the car windows to hold it down—and a smile on Mama's face.

How she loved that table.

Years later, when I was old enough to know how much my father loved Mama, I realized he would have carried that old table to Virginia on his back if she had asked him.

Mama's table made it to Virginia on top of the pink car, but the pink car lasted only a week before my father traded it in for a blue sedan.

CHAPTER 5

BACK WHEN WE MADE the Okies from *The Grapes of Wrath* with the table-on-top-of-the-car-move to Virginia, I was not yet two years old and had already moved five times. The move from Oklahoma to Virginia was my sixth move, fourth state, and fifth town. Moving came with my father's job. From one house to a better one down the street or even to another town if it was closer to the base. Closer to base was a priority since we had only one car, and Daddy had to have it to drive to work. So if we got a chance to get closer to base, we moved. Even if the house wasn't any better. Even if the house was worse.

The government was supposed to supply housing, but it never seemed to get a house supplied when you needed it. Housing was just one of the benefits the government promised and couldn't deliver. "The government, not the Marine Corps," Daddy would say. "The government is a mess and twenty years behind on paperwork, but Marines stick together and help each other out. The Marine Corps is a well-oiled machine. The government, well . . . that's another story."

He was always saying things like, "The government's promisin' mouth is about twenty years ahead of its deliverin' butt." (I was not allowed to say *butt* if it had two ts, but Daddy could.) Then he would turn around and defend the government's right to mess up with the same energy, saying, "But there isn't a better place on this earth to live 'cause I've been there and back again. We have to stand up straight and put our hands on our hearts and pledge to the government for which it stands with pride because our boys are dying for that flag over in . . ." Somewhere. I always forgot where they were dying. That was always changing anyway. Eventually, though, Daddy would get his orders, which meant we got ours too.

"I've got orders," he would announce.

Then Mama would ask, "Where to?" And they would both grin or groan, and our stuff would start to disappear into boxes.

I don't know where the orders came from. They just appeared, and then we would start to pack and next would come the movers. After the movers piled all our stuff onto a big moving truck, we would climb into the car and cross the country; when we reached our destination, we would rent whatever house was available and affordable. Or not affordable, which was usually the case. Whatever was empty when we got to where we were going was what we got. If we didn't find something pretty quick, the moving van would unload everything we had into a warehouse. Everyone in the Marine Corps knew that a warehouse always ate some your furniture. Sometimes all of your things vanished for weeks before surfacing—some pieces never to surface again.

Unloading everything into a warehouse, then reloading it all back onto a van—then unloading it once again when you finally got housing—was like an extra move and something to be avoided. "Three moves are equal to one good fire. Might as well trash it all and start over again," was a common shared military truth that Mama repeated every time we moved. Nobody we knew had a full set of furniture after a few moves. One move, you would lose a headboard. The next, an end table. Three-piece sectionals weren't *three* after a move or two. Military families traded stuff back and forth because whatever fit into your old house never fit into the next house anyway.

"Marine Corp chic—that's what you tell people when they ask how your house is decorated," Mama would say. Finding a house was tricky too. If you waited for a rental notice to appear in the paper, it was probably too late. The only sure way you could find a house was by word of mouth. Someone would get orders and call to tell you they were vacating their house. Someone was always leaving. Someone was always arriving. And then the shuffle would begin. One family would move out the front door while another family moved in the back door. Often at the same time.

Sometimes you had to move in with friends on base for a few days. Even if you didn't know them, they were your friends. Marines have a lot of friends. And bunk beds. Everyone has bunk beds.

The government paid for the moves from station to station, but moves from house to house were up to you, and the enlisted troops came first when it came to getting housing on base. Mama said that was only fair because the troops needed all the help they could get since the government didn't pay them enough money to starve with any dignity.

Marine families were always broke from moving.

"We'll manage," Mama would say. "The troops need to be first-come at military housing because it's a sure thing they'll be the first to die when the time comes." I don't know how Mama knew about the dying order of things, but she seemed to know.

The year after we left Oklahoma for Virginia, we moved two more times before we finally found a real house with a big backyard and a clothesline where we could hang the wash out to dry instead of draping wet things over the fence. And we got a dog, one that tore the clothes off our new clothesline until Mama explained the "Way of the Lord" to him. We also got a new sister, which was almost as exciting as getting a yard and a dog. We named the dog Feet and the sister Amy.

Feet stayed.

Amy didn't.

CHAPTER 6

ONE MINUTE, EVERYTHING was fine. The next, we were racing for the hospital—with Daddy trying to help Amy breathe. And then we waited. On a hard bench in a long, white hall, Daddy, Mama, Pat, and I sat in shared silence until a doctor came out, leaned over, and whispered something to my daddy, and then to my mama. Daddy put his head in his hands, and his shoulders began to tremble. He had always told us, "Marines don't cry," but now here he was crying. I didn't know what to do. Mama wrapped her arms around Pat and me and pulled us so close we could hardly breathe. We sat there, smothered in her arms. Mama looked numb. She didn't speak. There was only silence. And the sound of my father crying.

A week later, Pat began kindergarten. Daddy went back to work. Mama and I were left alone in an empty house. She took down the crib, folded and boxed baby clothes, and then took everything up to the attic.

Later I asked my sister, "Where did Amy go?"

"She went to heaven," Pat said.

"Didn't she like us? Was it my fault she left?"

"Mama said it was no one's fault. God just loaned her to us for a little while."

"Do you think we're loaned? Is God going to take us back too?"

My sister looked at me for a moment, then handed me her Barbie dolls. "Here, you can play with them while I'm at school," she told me.

Pat never let anyone play with her Barbies.

"And no, Beebe, we're not loaned. We belong here. We're staying."

After days and days of almost total silence, Mama woke me up one morning and said, "Beebe, hop out of bed and get dressed. Let's go looking."

"What for?"

"I don't know yet, but we need to get out of this house and do something."

She was smiling. She looked like my mama again.

We packed a lunch, dropped Pat off at school, and Mama and I went looking. Every morning, that became our routine. Mama would run a load of wash, hang it out on the line to dry, straighten up the kitchen, and off we would go . . . looking.

One morning, I asked her, "Where're we going today?"

"Pirate's Den in Alexandria. I hear they have old furniture," she said.

Most days, we came back from our looking trips empty-handed, but on that day, we found a large, round oak dining table that Mama decided to buy. Our next-door neighbor cut the pedestal down and turned it into a coffee table for us.

"Perfect place for my feet," Daddy said upon seeing it.

"I like it!" Pat said. "You and Mama did good. I can color and do my school stuff on it."

Antique shops, flea markets, yard sales. Where we went didn't matter to me. I had never had Mama all to myself before. I felt special.

"What do you think about these candlesticks, Beebe?" she asked me one day as we rummaged through a table in a junk shop.

"They're pretty." I answered. "I like them 'cause they shine."

"I agree," she said. "They'll be perfect!"

We ate supper that evening with sterling-silver candlesticks on the gateleg table, with candlelight flickering and casting a glow over the four of us: Mama, Daddy, Pat, and me.

During a lull, Daddy asked Pat how she liked kindergarten.

"It's okay." She shrugged her shoulders.

"Give it some time. Maybe it will get better," he said. He turned to me and asked, "What are you and your mama doing every day while Pat's in school?"

"Looking," I said. "We look. We look for pretty things. We eat lunch in the park. We have fun."

Daddy nodded, then reached across the table and took my mama's hand. "And you? Are you okay?"

Mama looked at him for a moment before she spoke.

"No. Not really," she finally said. "I don't even know what that means right now."

Before Daddy could respond, she added, "I've heard good things sometimes come from bad. I'm not sure that's true, but I've never had much time to spend with Beebe before. I think she likes being an only child all day while Pat's at school." (I was christened Rebecca, but almost everyone called me Becky. Save for my mother. She always called me Beebe.)

Mama and Daddy were now lost in each other's eyes. Daddy smiled and squeezed her hand. It was as if Pat and I weren't even there.

CHAPTER 7

THE MARINE CORPS MUST have forgotten where they had put my daddy because they didn't move him again for two years. That was nice because when he didn't move, we didn't move either. Instead, every morning, Daddy went to work and Pat went to school. Every evening, the two of them returned home, and we all had supper on the gateleg table. Just like a normal family. Whatever that means. Normal or not, we had settled in.

One year passed, then two. And then, just when I was getting used to Virginia, the orders came again, and out came the boxes.

Mama had a unique prepacking routine she went through whenever we moved. Pat and I knew it like we knew all her routines. But this time, right in the middle of it, she up and sent me and Pat to the neighbor's house to stay, saying that she was going to get caught up on some things.

"If you are good, you can stay and play for a couple of days," she told us. "It will be more fun for you two. I have to sort things here and get everything into boxes, and that will be easier without the two of you underfoot. I also need to get some things from the PX and . . ." Her voice faded off before she could finish her sentence.

Her plan sounded good to me. Pat and I hated to go to the PX. Before she dropped us off at the neighbors', Mama reminded us to be sure to say please and thank-you, to use a napkin when we ate, to act civilized, and to not cause any trouble. Mama was always telling us to act civilized. According to her, we acted like little savages most of the time. I don't think she ever meant Pat when she said this. Pat is quiet and well mannered. No one would ever mistake my sister for a savage, and besides, Mama always looked at me when she said this.

When we returned from our stay at the neighbors' house, Mama had bought us toothbrushes, green-and-white-striped toothpaste, socks, new underwear, and a little brother. That was the best thing she'd ever brought home from the PX. He was almost as good as a dog. We stuck him into a drawer full of sheets where he could sleep, and we kept right on packing.

Our new brother's name was Kenneth Scott Jacks, which was an awfully big name for such a little baby. We all called him Scooter or Scotty except for my daddy, who always called him Sam. And there was a reason for that. My daddy's name is Ken, but the men at work call him by his first name, which changes every few years. When I was born it was Captain. The year Mama got Scooter from the PX in Virginia, it was Major. And the year after we moved to Beaufort, it changed again—this time to Colonel. Daddy was adamant that Scooter would not carry his name. "Enough people in my family named Ken already," Daddy told Mama. "If this baby is a boy, we'll name him *David Scott*, not *Kenneth Scott*."

Mama had disagreed. "Your name ought to belong to your son if we ever have a son. Your sister and brother shouldn't have used your name for their little boys just because you had girls first. And anyway, we aren't going to call him Ken, we're going to call him Scott. So it's just a formality to name him Kenneth Scott."

But Daddy wouldn't budge. "No more kids in this family named Ken," he said. "David Scott is a fine name for a boy. We'll call him Scott. Or David. But not Ken or Kenneth or Kenny."

That was the end of that as far as he was concerned.

Before he was born, the compromise was my brother's name would be David Scott. After he was born, it wasn't, because Mama was the one who filled out the birth certificate. I don't know what Mama thought would happen when she filled out my brother's name on that birth certificate as Kenneth Scott. I guess she figured Daddy would never see it since he was gone so much. She probably counted on being the one who would open the mail when the official birth certificate came. Maybe she actually thought nobody else but her would ever see it. She would be the one to enroll my brother in school when he got big enough to go. She would be the one to take him to the clinic to get his shots. I'm sure she was probably thinking, "Who looks at a birth certificate anyway?"

The day my baby brother's birth certificate arrived in the mail, however, Daddy came home early. He brought the mail in and opened it. I don't remember him saying a word at the time. Come suppertime, however, after he took his regular place at the table, he laid the big envelope by his plate, blessed our food, and then announced that someone had surely made a big mistake because he knew his sweet wife would never get something as important as a boy's name wrong on his official birth certificate. He handed the envelope in question to Mama and asked, "How do you think this happened? The military usually gets its paperwork right."

Mama smiled. "Well now, I wonder how that happened?"

Daddy didn't respond, and Mama now looked a little puzzled. "I guess I was probably still under the anesthesia when they asked me for his name, and I probably just, you know, probably remembered that we had talked about a boy having his father's name. And probably I just told them his name was Kenneth Scott. Probably."

"You didn't get there in time for anesthetic," my daddy reminded her, but the wrinkles around his eyes looked as if he was trying not to laugh. "And don't you think that's an awful lot of *probablys*?"

A silence fell over the room as we waited to hear Mama's answer. After a minute or two, when she didn't reply, Daddy said, "Well, since no one can agree on what this boy's name should be, I'm going to call him Sam." And he did. From then on.

For the rest of my life, I never once heard my father call my brother anything but Sam. "Where's Sam?" he would ask. Or "Beebe, what have you and Sam been up to today?" As it turned out, nobody else ever called him Scott either. And as for me, the only question I ever had about that whole conversation that night was why would Mama think someone had given her anesthesia at the PX?

The story of how my brother got his name became another of Daddy's favorite stories, one he especially liked to tell when we had company. The bigger the crowd, the better. Mama always told him to hush and quit embarrassing her, but he never did. Everybody would be laughing by the time Daddy had finished, and the story always ended the same way: "You know, folks, the Corps can take a beach, a desert, or a mountain, but one little woman can stop a Marine in his tracks every time, so you better take your friends along if you try to go to war with a woman. Most cussed creature God ever made."

CHAPTER 8

THE DAY WE LEFT VIRGINIA, the moving vans arrived a little early. But the movers were still loading our boxes onto the truck when Daddy hollered, "Get in the car—now! We're off to Beaufort, South Carolina." Daddy only said *now* when it was time to hit the road.

Mama laid our new baby brother in a basket on the floorboard of the back seat between my feet, and the dog flopped onto the middle of the seat beside me. Luckily, he—my brother, not the dog—came from the PX in a small size because our dog, Feet, was huge, the car was crowded, and Daddy said he wasn't going anywhere without the dog. What a relief. I had not wanted us to have to choose between my brother and the dog. I would have felt real bad choosing the dog.

Pat already had her nose buried in a book and her free arm around Feet, scratching his ears, which made his hind leg jiggle and twitch, bumping me at every jiggle. The ice chest sat between her feet on the floorboard. It had a slow steady leak, which was good because that way we didn't have to worry about a water bowl for the dog. He kept the entire back floorboard lapped clean, licking up water and crumbs as well as drool from my brother's face.

On the trip from Virginia to South Carolina, Mama said my job was to regularly check Scooter to see if he was wet and needed to be changed, which was difficult to tell between the leaky ice chest and the dog's slurping. They kept everything in the backseat damp. Long trips are boring with nothing to do but check for wet diapers, so I decided to teach him all the weird faces that I knew. My brother, not the dog.

Everything was going pretty well until it came time to change the first diaper. Scooter was rigged up different from me and my sister, and when we took his diaper off, he just let 'er rip, spraying the ceiling of the car like a fountain, which kept my daddy in stitches, but didn't amuse Mama at all.

"Put a diaper over the top of him before you take the other one off," Mama suggested. "Or hand him over the seat to me, and I'll take care of him." That, however, was out of the question because the back seat and floor were packed so tight neither Pat nor I could move, much less lift a dripping ten-pound wiggler. All in all, it was a soggy trip.

Something wonderful, however, did happen on our move from Virginia to Beaufort, South Carolina—God spoke to the government, and we got base housing the same day we arrived. We had never had military housing on base before. We had never before had housing of any sort on the first day in a new town.

I don't think the government had a clue how bad God had messed up their paperwork because we didn't even have to shuffle from one place to another, and we didn't have to stay in a motel at all. We drove right through the air-station gate and up to the base housing office. Daddy got the keys, and we were standing in our new living room when the moving van arrived that afternoon: A perfect house on the corner next to the woods and a block away from the water. Heaven on earth.

We opened the boxes Mama had labeled "Sheets and Pillows" and slept on our own pillows in our own beds that very first night. It was home from the first minute we walked in the door. The only big difference between Virginia and South Carolina was the noise of the jets screaming overhead. All day and all night. A constant roar.

CHAPTER 9

IN LAUREL BAY, WHICH WAS the name of the Beaufort military housing section, some of the families centered their lives around the beach, some around the bowling alley or the baseball field. Other families never adjusted to the move and rarely came out of their houses at all. Except for the men. The men left every morning for the air station dressed in olive green or khaki, with an assortment of brightly colored ribbons, medals, and wings on their chests.

Our family centered our life around supper at the cherry table—and the church. We always went to church. Every Sunday, rain or shine. "No need to miss," my daddy told us the first Sunday after we moved to Laurel Bay. "We're not sick, and everybody's got their Sunday shoes unpacked. So put 'em on, and we'll go to town and check out what the Baptists down south are doing today. See if God knows where we landed."

The town of Beaufort had one fancy church. Two stories with a balcony and old straight-backed wooden pews, with gates that had little locks on them. I guess the locks were to let you know it wasn't your pew if you didn't have the key. The church had served as a hospital during the Civil War, and the wounded men had scratched their names into the wood on the walls of the balcony, leaving messages for their loved ones in case they never made it home. The building survived the war, and the congregation left the soldiers' names where they were, scars in the wood to remember their fallen.

We went to that church only that once. We hadn't been there long when a black Marine pilot and his family came in. Suddenly, the ushers decided there weren't any more seats available, though anyone could see there were. The next week, we found another Baptist church. One that had seats for everyone.

Down south in the sixties, military people weren't much better thought of than black folk. Military folk, black folk, and the migrant gypsies who picked the crops. White trash, black trash, and traveling trash. We were spared most of the indignities and trouble black folks unfairly suffered—but we weren't treated like regular folk either, and the locals made it clear they didn't think much of us. I didn't let it bother me, but I never got used to people being divided up by color like crayons.

CHAPTER 10

Pryor, Oklahoma
2010

I PUT MY CHILDHOOD JOURNAL back into the drawer of the bureau. Once you start to think about the past, there is no good place to stop. I had never written much in my journal as a child—or very often for that matter. How much does a child have to say? It was all the words between the lines—all that I hadn't written—that now occupied my thoughts.

Before I shut the bottom drawer of the dresser, I raked a scattering of seashells into a pile so I could decide what to do with them later.

As I scooped them up, my heart skipped a beat.

Underneath the seashells was an envelope.

A little girl with a million small treasures from Beaufort had chosen to save so few of them. Some seashells, her journal, and . . . the letter.

The envelope was addressed to my mother. From my father. Inside was a single sheet of official paper from the U.S. Marine Corps. I felt sad for the child that used to be me. A child who had been alone in the silence that had come with the letter.

Even a child knows silence when she hears it.

CHAPTER 11

THE DAY I CAME HOME FROM catching the biggest crab ever with my little brother, the letter was already sitting on the old gateleg table, unopened. Mama must have left it there when she brought in the rest of the mail. The address on the envelope read:

Mrs. E. K. Jacks
142 Birch Drive
Laurel Bay, S.C.

The return address said Lt. Col. E. Ken Jacks at the same Birch Drive address, which was strange. Why would Daddy send a letter to our house, to Mama, when he saw her every morning and every night and could have just as easily handed it to her? Why write a letter to someone living in the same house? Why write a letter in the first place?

"Mama, we're home!" I yelled as the screen door slammed behind me. "Me and Scooter got crabs!" For some reason, Mama always chuckled when I said that. "You got a letter!"

I knew Mama knew she had a letter. She was the one who had brought in the mail.

I tried again, "There's a letter here on the table. Did you see it?"

Silence.

"You want me to bring it to you?"

More silence.

"It hasn't been opened yet!"

My mother was, as I said, famously uncurious. When she got a package, she might leave it unopened for days, and then say something unreasonable like, "I'm saving it for when I need a reward. I'll get these dishes done and the washing machine running. Then I'll sit down with a cup of tea while I relax and open my package." Or letter. Or present. Or whatever. She always delays and waits. I never understood it. What's the point of waiting? The work never gets done, and by the time she gets through doing whatever she is doing, it's usually too late. She falls into bed for the night without ever getting to the good stuff.

Mama believes in saving the best for last all the time, which is the dumbest rule of all the rules she has. It's agonizing. I always do the best thing first so that I'm always doing the best thing. It's really the only sensible way to do things—since the thing that is left over after you do the best thing then becomes the best thing. I like my system. I got it from my daddy. Mama is fond of saying that's also the reason I never get around to doing the other things on my list, things like making my bed or taking a bath. Which I suppose, is true, but then there are only so many hours in a day.

"Mama, how come Daddy wrote you a letter?" I hollered.

Silence.

"How come you haven't opened it?"

More silence.

I waited for her to answer me as long as I could stand it and then shouted: "You want me to open it for you?"

I knew the answer to that would be no as well, but still thought it was important to try. Sometimes grown-ups ignore you when you want to talk, and sometimes they talk to you when you want them to ignore you. This was one of those first kind of times. Truth is, I wasn't sure Mama had even heard me; so I went looking for her. I found her in the kitchen leaning over the sink peeling potatoes and staring out the window. She stood so still, I knew that she wasn't looking at anything in particular. Every little while, she would take a deep breath and pick up another potato. Sometimes grown-ups go off into a world of their own, and you have to wait until they come back. And from the way she was staring off into space, it looked like she wasn't coming back anytime soon.

"Mama?"

Silence.

Yep, wherever she was, Mama couldn't hear me.

I don't give up easy, but this was one of those times when even I knew I was wasting my breath. Still, an unopened letter was too much for a little kid like me to bear for very long. I had to know what was in the envelope and why my mother wouldn't open it—even if I had to open it myself, which I knew I most probably wouldn't do because that would most probably be a sin. Most probably.

Sin is a funny thing. Sometimes you don't know that you did one until later when you get into trouble, and by then it's too late. You might as well go ahead and do what you're thinking about doing—and take your punishment if it happens to turn out later that what you did was a sin. I'm sure Mama wouldn't agree with my reasoning as far as the sinning goes, but since she has a forgiving heart, I figured if it came to that it couldn't hurt.

I put the letter back on the table where I had found it.

Unopened.

But my heart wasn't in it.

CHAPTER 12

A FTER MAMA FINISHED PEELING and dicing the potatoes, she put them in a pot on the stove to boil and got the skillet out—a black number-eight, cast-iron chicken fryer. She used it every night for something: Fried chicken, fried okra, stir-fried corn. Southern fried—that's how everybody cooked before they learned to worry about what all that fried food did to your innards.

Our kitchen always smelled of onions and spice and bananas. My favorite room in the house. The oven gave off warmth in the winter. The blender and the mixer made wonderful whirring noises. I even liked the way ice clink-clanked when you put it into a glass and the way tea gurgled when you poured it over ice. I like noises. And I loved our kitchen, especially when I got to sit on the counter and watch my mother cook.

If I wasn't in the kitchen with Mama, I could usually be found outside playing or waiting for my daddy to come home from work—from Japan, from Spain, from Cuba, from wherever. His life was exciting. He went to interesting places all the time. We did not. Mama, Pat, me, and Scooter had to stay at home because the President never invited us to go anywhere. Daddy said that if the Marines had wanted you to have a wife or children, they would have issued them to you when you joined up. Mama told him that wasn't funny.

My favorite thing to do in the kitchen was mixing stuff. I liked to get my hands into gooey things. Mama didn't. She was neat. Very, very neat. When Mama cooked, nothing was ever out of place, everything was measured just so, and seldom did she spill anything. After she used a pan or a bowl, she would rinse it out and put it into the dishwasher right then, so that when dinner was over, there was nothing to clean up but our plates, glasses, and silverware. When Mama and I cooked together, Mama would always end up saying, *Beebe, you be careful. Do you hear me? Don't make a mess that you and I will have to clean up. Okay?* Actually, I never had to clean up. Mama said, *You and I*, but she always cleaned up the kitchen herself. There's clean, and then there's Mama's clean, the latter of which did not include me helping her.

"Beebe, please call Pat in to help you set the table, then go out and check the driveway. Let me know when your father arrives so I can start the gravy," Mama said.

I did as she said and went to get Pat, then commenced checking the driveway every few minutes for Daddy. Meanwhile, Pat got out the plates. I folded napkins, and then placed the silverware, sugar bowl, and the salt and pepper shakers in the middle of the table. We seldom used place mats for dinner. Mama would say, *I'd just as soon wash a tablecloth if I'm going to wash something. As far as I'm concerned, we don't need either one. Cherrywood's too pretty to cover up, and Scooter's going to spill something anyway, so why make more work washing and ironing?*

Truth was, Mama didn't mind washing and ironing tablecloths or anything else for that matter—she just liked the way the wood looked. The wax was so thick on the table that the water beaded up like drops of dew if something spilled on it. And someone was always spilling something. Especially Scooter, who has been known to spill things on purpose; you could tell if his intentions weren't pure if he giggled when he did it.

On this evening, while Mama finished up dinner in the kitchen, I moved the letter and the silver candelabra off the cherry table, shaking the envelope to be sure there wasn't anything inside that rattled. There wasn't. The envelope, however, did look as if it might pop open with a little help, so I wiggled my finger under the flap to be sure the seal was still stuck. It was. Disappointed, I told myself God was probably trying to keep me from sinning. I gave up and propped the unopened letter against the sugar bowl where Mama would be sure to see it, while my sister put ice in the glasses for tea. Iced tea. Winter and summer, all year-round.

When we were done, I returned to the end of the driveway to wait for my daddy in my usual spot on the lawn. All the houses on our street were cookie-cutter military and looked exactly the same, and I didn't want him to get lost.

Supper that night was larruping: Chicken-fried steak, smashed potatoes, gravy, green peas, and sliced mangoes. We had never had mango before. Daddy said he got 'dicted to them while in the Philippines. Over there, he ate mangoes every morning for breakfast and every evening for dessert. "Mangoes don't taste exactly right stateside," he told us, "but any mango is better than no mango at all. They are God's greatest single achievement. After your mama, of course."

And then he winked at us.

Mama rolled her eyes, but she was smiling.

I will always remember the night I had my first mango and tried to open the letter. And one remember always seems to lead to another. My next remember was the prayer I said when I went to bed that night:

> *Now God. You need to listen to me.*
> *It's really hard having a mother who isn't curious.*
> *Would you please do something about that?*
> *Because I need to know what's in that letter.*
> *Thank you.*
> *Amen.*

CHAPTER 13

IN SEPTEMBER, MY SISTER STARTED second grade. Scooter and I spent most of our days playing outside or going to the beach. My job was to watch my brother and keep him out of trouble—or at least from getting hurt, but since he was determined to do both, it was a difficult job. One afternoon while playing leapfrog with some of the neighborhood kids, I made it worse. Scooter was about to jump and I gave him a push. He went flying over three or four kids, and the next thing I heard was a snap. And then a screech.

"I's broke! I's broke my neck!" Scooter yelled.

My heart stopped. This was all my fault. "Someone go tell my mama to call an ambulance!" I yelled. I sure didn't want to be the one to tell her that Scooter thought his neck was broke. Especially since I was pretty sure I was the one who had broke it.

"What happened?" Mama asked as she came out the door. She seemed calm, but then, she was always calm in a crisis.

"We were playing leapfrog," I said, "and somebody gave Scooter a little boost and he crash-landed on his head."

I held my breath and waited to hear what Mama would say, which turned out to be nothing. Instead, she leaned over my brother with a worried look and asked him where he hurt. She didn't ask who the somebody was that had given Scooter the boost. What a relief.

The ambulance drove up as the school bus dropped off my sister.

"Is he going to die?" Pat asked Mama, then turning to me. "What happened?" I retold my story, only this time including who the mysterious somebody was.

"Sometimes, Becky, you're a certified *idgit*. You've probably gone and killed your own brother!" Pat said, shaking her head in disbelief. At that, I began to hiccup—a habit of mine when trying not to cry.

"Oh, don't cry," Pat said. "I'm sorry I called you an idgit. Maybe he will live. I'm sure you didn't *mean* to kill him."

Meanwhile, Mama remained knelt beside Scooter, who, it must be said, was *still* screaming at the top of his lungs, as the medic tried to check him out. The final verdict? Scooter's neck was fine, but his collarbone was definitely broken.

The medics lifted Scooter onto a stretcher, slid him into the ambulance, and then waited as we all piled in. Pat sat up front, and me and Mama climbed into the back with my brother. The flashing lights and screaming wail of the ambulance turned the trip to the hospital into a fabulous adventure. Like I said, I like noises. Scooter does too. We hadn't gone far before he had stopped yelling and started grinning. Mama was so relieved that his neck wasn't broken—and grateful that he had stopped yelling—she never did ask who had boosted him and caused the ruckus in the first place. I sure wasn't going to tell her. Sometimes it's better to keep your mouth shut.

"There's not much you can do for a broken collarbone," the doctor told my mother. "Try to keep him from moving his arm and shoulder for a while. I've taped him up, but you can't set a broken collarbone."

The doctor obviously did not know my brother. Keeping Scooter from moving his arm and shoulder would be nigh impossible, tape or no tape. About the only thing that would keep my little brother still would be the pain.

We all went home in the ambulance, and Mama put Scooter down for a nap. She was always saying she would like to break one of our necks, but she seemed glad that my brother hadn't broken his. She went to the kitchen and began to make cookies as if nothing had happened. "Girls, please come here. Hop up on the counter and taste this cookie dough for me." Mama held out two spoons. One for me, and one for Pat.

Mama nearly always makes cookies when something good happens. She also makes cookies when something bad happens. Making cookies is her remedy for everything.

"What do you think?" Mama asked. "Does it taste right? Maybe I better taste it too." She stuck her finger into the batter.

"It's perfect!" Pat declared. "You need to get a spoon, Mama."

When we bake cookies, we always end up eating too much cookie dough, spoonful after spoonful, until Mama finally calls a halt to it only to then say, "I bet we get sick, but just one more bite." It is only after that last spoonful that we start to drop blobs of whatever dough remains onto a cookie sheet.

On this night, we formed a little ring around the bowl and helped ourselves spoonful by spoonful to the batter until finally Mama said, "We need to leave a few cookies for your brother when he wakes up. It might keep him still for a little while."

It wouldn't, but then she already knew that.

For once, I didn't argue. I still felt bad about the push.

Mama got a cookie sheet out and started spooning the last of the batter onto it. I smashed each of the blobs of dough flat with a fork, and Pat put them in the oven. Peanut butter is our favorite cookie, but any kind of cookie will do. Most of the time, we eat so much of the cookie dough that we have to make another batch.

CHAPTER 14

I STARTED FIRST GRADE THE YEAR AFTER we moved to Beaufort. School was awful—unnecessary as well, because I already knew how to read. But I had to go. It was the law. If you live in America and you're six years old, they lock you up in late August or early September and throw away the key until May. Every morning now, Scooter and I spent it waiting for the school bus. The bus would stop in front of our house. I would get on, wave goodbye to my brother, and he'd go back into the house to do whatever it was Scooter did to pass the time until his sisters returned after school.

Except for the day we lost him. On that day, Scooter waited for me to get on the bus and wave but he didn't go back inside the house.

Instead, right after my bus pulled out, a second bus drove up. When that driver saw Scooter standing at the curb, he stopped and yelled for him to get on the bus. So Scooter got on. It wasn't Scooter's fault he got lost that day. He was just a little kid; he usually did what people told him to do. He usually only had a problem with the things people *didn't* tell him not to do, like *do not get on a school bus*. Nobody could possibly think of all the millions of things my brother should have been told not to do. The list was endless.

After all the excitement of losing Scooter was over, one of the girls who rode the second bus to school that day told me what had happened. "Your brother got on the bus and sat down," she said, "and when the bus stopped at the school, everyone got off, so he did too. I didn't see him after that, but one of my friends said he went in and sat down in one of the classrooms at a desk as if he belonged there—so nobody paid him any mind."

Scooter did look like a first-grader. He was as tall as the other first-graders, even though he was only four years old. He could have stayed at school all day like a normal kid if he had only kept his mouth shut. Military kids came and went, so sometimes teachers didn't have a clue as to who was whom, or who was new. Families transferred in and out all the time. Teachers came and went as well because most of them were military wives. Sometimes by the end of the year, you didn't end up with anyone in the room who had started at the beginning of the year. Teachers or kids. So it wasn't unusual that this teacher didn't know my brother didn't belong there or that he was lost at first.

Before long, though, she did realize something was off. He didn't know his last name, his address, or much of anything else. The teacher called the principal, and the two of them dragged Scooter around from room to room until someone recognized him and said that he wasn't old enough to be in school. No one knew his real name because everyone always called him Scooter. Somebody told the principal that he was fun to play with because he laughed a lot and did what everyone told him to do even if it was stupid or dangerous. Eventually, the principal called the Beaufort police to see if a child had been reported missing. While they waited on an answer, they fed Scooter lunch and tried to figure out who he was. That's where I found him, in the cafeteria—eating Tater Tots and blowing bubbles into his milk carton.

"What's my brother doing here?" I asked.

Nobody seemed to know. So you could say Scooter was found before I even knew that he was lost. The same could not be said for Mama. Our mother knew he was lost. All morning. When the school finally reached her, she and the military police were about ready to drag the bay for his body. The MPs had been looking for Scooter for hours, thinking that perhaps he had wandered down to the beach and drowned or wandered across the street into the woods and gotten lost. Nobody thought about him getting onto a school bus and going to school.

"He's ours, and we want him back," Mama told the school principal when she went to get him.

"Well, you need to keep an eye on him or he's likely to catch a bus to California someday," the principal said with a chuckle.

Mama did not laugh.

That evening, by the time my father had landed, debriefed, and exchanged his flight suit for his uniform to come home, everything was over, and Scooter was back at home. Daddy dismissed the entire thing and said, "Nothing exciting ever happens when I'm around. I think you girls just make these things up for my entertainment."

CHAPTER 15

IN LAUREL BAY, WE LIVED NEXT-DOOR to a nice doctor who was Jewish and his family. His wife, Jeanette, was not Jewish—she was Catholic, which added a little religious spice to their lives, according to my mother. Jeanette Golfeder was drop-dead gorgeous. Magazine-cover beautiful. Their four-year-old son, Andy, took after her. His father, Doctor Philip Golfeder, or Dr. Phil, as we called him, was not beautiful. He resembled a friendly gnome. Everyone in my family liked Dr. Phil a lot. I liked him because he didn't treat me like a stupid little kid.

Dr. Phil was a neurosurgeon. He kept brains in big jars in his hall closet arranged in order according to size. Small brain to large. I never heard him say what kind of brains they were. I wasn't sure I wanted to know. I wasn't the only one made uneasy by them. I heard Andy's mom say more than once that she would leave Dr. Phil for good if he ever opened that particular closet door while she was cooking dinner.

"You and Andy can look at the brains all you want to after we eat, but if you open that closet door while I'm cooking, I'm leaving, and you won't get supper," she would say. We kept coats and the vacuum cleaner in our hall closet. Boring.

Everyone agreed that Dr. Phil was brilliant. In the evening, he would sit on the front porch of his house holding the local newspaper in one hand and reading what he said wasn't very interesting news, while tying knots in a piece of string with the other hand behind his back. "The Beaufort paper never prints anything interesting. I don't think these southerners know that New York or the rest of the world is on the map," he would complain. "As a matter of fact, you know what I think I'll do, Rebecca? I think I'll order us the Philadelphia paper."

Dr. Phil always called me Rebecca, which he said was an upstanding biblical name. According to him, my name had belonged to the Jews first, but he said he guessed he didn't mind if I used it. Many an evening, Dr. Phil and I would sit on the Golfeders' porch swing and read the local newspaper. At some point, he would holler to his wife, "Jeanette, would you bring Rebecca and me a glass of tea please? We are having a serious discussion about the news of the day!"

Jeanette would bring the tea, plop Andy down beside me, and tell him, "Listen to your dad and Becky. You might learn something. And Phil, darling, you don't have to yell. I'm not deaf. But if you keep up your hollering, you can get your own tea."

She always seemed serious when she said it, but as long as I knew them, Dr. Phil kept on hollering and Jeanette kept right on bringing us tea. As time went by, however, it became clear that Dr. Phil wasn't going to let the idea of changing newspapers go. "We need to read about something besides quilting bees," he said. "I am tired of reading about church suppers, Rotary Club meetings, and the Masons. We need to find out what's going on in the rest of the world."

"That's not the only things they print," I told him. "They also print marriage announcements and babies that just got born, ladies having tea, birthdays, and dead people."

"That's exactly what I'm talking about," Dr. Phil said. "Beaufort doesn't seem very interested in what's going on in the rest of the world. Up north appears to mean Charleston, and down south, Savannah. I'm going to order us a real newspaper to read."

That was fine by me. I was bored with the Beaufort paper anyway. Dr. Phil was right; the news in it was the same every single day.

Although I did think it was probably a good thing that nobody from Beaufort overheard us, as I was pretty sure they would not have appreciated Dr. Phil's opinion of *their* opinion of what qualified as news worth reading in a local newspaper.

While it was true that nothing much ever seemed to happen in Beaufort, unusual things did occasionally occur on base—or at least in base housing and sometimes even in our own house. My older sister, Pat, had a tiny painted turtle she kept in a big, flat bowl on our coffee table. She had put pebbles and seashells in the bottom of the bowl and a rock in the middle so the turtle could climb up on it and get out of the water. One day when Andy was at our house with his mom, the turtle crawled up on top of the rock. Andy reached in, picked the turtle up by the tail, and popped it into his mouth. He swallowed the turtle whole—painted shell and all.

"Andy ate the turtle," I told Jeanette and Mama.

"He ate *what?*" Mama and Jeanette said in unison.

"Pat's turtle," I said. "He ate it. Headfirst."

They didn't seem all that surprised. Or worried.

"Well, I guess that means he's had his protein for the day," Jeanette said. "What do you think? Have any of your kids ever eaten a live turtle? Do I need to call Phil?"

"What's Phil going to do?" my mama said. "He's a brain surgeon." She wrinkled her nose. "Ugh. Poor turtle."

"Yeah," Jeanette said. "What a way to go. Swallowed."

"Only way it could hurt Andy is if it decided to bite him on the way down," my mama said.

"Doesn't have teeth—all it could have done is give him a good nip," Jeanette agreed. "Anyway, it's probably a goner by now."

They returned to their tea. Nothing rattles military wives. After Andy and his mother left, I asked Mama, "What are we going to tell Pat about her turtle when she gets home from school?"

"Oh, mercy! I hadn't thought about that. Maybe she won't notice."

"You know she will," I said. "She'll be all upset that her turtle is gone, and it will break her heart if she finds out Andy ate it."

"You're right, of course. What was I thinking? Round up your brother. We have to go to town and get another turtle before Pat gets home. Do you think she'll be able to tell the difference?"

"Maybe not," I said. That wasn't exactly true. I knew Pat would absolutely be able to tell the difference, but it would have made Mama feel bad if I had said so. Knowing Pat, she had probably memorized the color and position of every spot on her turtle's back. Turns out I was right about that too.

"Where's my turtle?" Pat asked when she got in from school that afternoon. "And where did this strange turtle come from?"

She held up Mama's replacement. Before Mama could reply, I confessed. "I'm real sorry, Pat; your turtle is gone. Andy ate him, and Mama felt so bad about it that she got you another one. She hoped you wouldn't notice." Mama had always told me to tell the truth, but this was also one of those times that no other good explanation as to how Pat's turtle had vanished came to mind.

"Andy ate my turtle?" Pat squeaked.

What could I possibly say to make it better? Nothing, it seemed. Pat started to cry, and that's when I decided to give her a hug. I'm not much of a hugger, but this seemed like a good time to practice.

"I'm sorry about your turtle, Pat, but I'm sure he didn't suffer. It was over real quick," I said.

Who knows whether that was true or not. I would run it by God later. It was just a kinda-sorta fib. Not a real lie. Kinda-sorta. Like when I told Mama that maybe Pat wouldn't notice that the turtle was different, when I knew for a fact that Pat would know the difference the second she saw the replacement.

CHAPTER 16

I F YOU WANTED DR. PHIL TO TALK to you, you had to hold up your end of the conversation. He always talked to me as if I was grown-up and had a brain. That's why when he complained about the Beaufort newspaper, I said, "Maybe they don't care much about what's going on in the rest of the world because they've got it so perfect down here, and they don't want to mess it up with bad news. Maybe it's because all the news in other papers is about murder and war and elections and Congress and stuff like that."

"Well, Rebecca, you're probably right," he said. "I need to stop complaining about it and instead take action. The obvious solution is to get another newspaper for us to read before my brain turns to mush. I'll take care of that after supper."

Sometimes when we read the newspaper together, Dr. Phil would ask Andy and me to hold it so he could read it aloud to us and still have both of his hands free to tie knots behind his back. Andy would sit on one side of his father and I would sit on the other. It was difficult not to jiggle the newspaper, and sometimes Andy and I jiggled the paper so much that Dr. Phil would miss a word in an article, and I would correct him. That's how he found out I could already read.

"How about you read the paper to us, Rebecca, and I'll tie knots," he said. So I read. Andy listened. And Dr. Phil tied knots. One evening I asked him, "Why do you tie knots behind your back? Why don't you tie them in front, where you can see what you're doing?"

"Well, Rebecca, I've got to know how to tie knots over my head, upside down, and in my sleep. I've got to be able to tie them with my eyes open or my eyes shut, because sometimes when I am working inside a brain, I can't see my fingers. Because sometimes I'm in a spot where there is room only for two fingers. Sometimes only one. So I practice. And someday, I'm hoping I can go back to Philadelphia and become a real neurosurgeon."

Before Dr. Phil could go to Philadelphia, however, I came down with a dread disease. Thankfully, Dr. Phil was still our neighbor. Mama called Jeanette in the middle of the night in a panic. It was so unlike my mother. Mama did not panic. "Becky's turned a funny color," she told Jeanette. "She can't drink anything and her face is swollen. Ken is gone; could you wake Phil? I'll unlock the front door so he can get in. Hurry, Jeanette! Tell him please hurry!" Whatever I had must be bad, because like I said, Mama never got in a panic. Ever. Military wives do not panic.

Dr. Phil came running over to our house, still in his pajamas with Jeanette right behind him. He took one look at me and called the emergency room on base to see who was on duty. Then he said, "Rebecca, you have a dread disease, but we are going to try to fix it at the hospital." He turned to my mother. "Call an ambulance while I change clothes."

Dr. Phil rode with me in the ambulance. Mama followed in the car, going way too fast, with an MP right behind her, red lights flashing. I figured she would get a ticket, but when we reached the hospital, the MP helped her out of the car and even parked it for her.

"Hey, wasn't that fun!" Mama said. She was holding my hand tight as they got me on a stretcher and rolled me into the emergency room. "Let's get you inside and find out what's going on so we can go home and put you back to bed."

Mama always had a way of making bad stuff not so scary. But she looked scared and so did Dr. Phil, which was scary to me.

To make matters worse, no one in a military family is allowed to get sick in the middle of the night. The military won't let you. But when I got the dread disease, I got it right smack-dab in the middle of the night, which was a huge problem because the military's rule is that you have to get sick in the daytime. First you make an appointment, and then you wait a week. Then on the day of your appointment, you wait some more in the waiting room before you see a nurse and find out if you are sick enough to see a doctor. You might die before you ever see a doctor. So you want to never, ever get sick at night. Even a little kid like me knew that.

Dr. Phil, however, wasn't like the other doctors at the clinic on base. Within minutes, he had two doctors in the emergency room helping him punch holes in me and running my blood down the hall to feed to the vampires.

Andy was the one who had told me about the vampires that lived in the hospital lab. "They take your blood and put it in tubes, and then they suck it out of the tubes and eat it for dinner," he said. "My papa told me so. Papa knows everything about blood and guts and stuff."

When I told Mama, she said Andy had an active imagination for a boy his age, although what he said about the vampires made sense to me. That night in the emergency room, the doctors took enough blood out of my arm to feed a town of vampires.

CHAPTER 17

"IT'S STEVENS-JOHNSON syndrome," I overheard Dr. Phil tell my mother. "It's rare, and the prognosis isn't encouraging. You need to get hold of Ken."

Dr. Phil explained to Mama that my capillaries were breaking down and causing me to bruise, turning me black and blue and a scary shade of purple. He didn't say how long it would take before I turned white again. He also didn't say that most people with the *sin-drome* didn't turn white again. They turned dead.

I didn't know the word *prognosis*, but there was a little kid on our street named *Steven Johnson*, and I knew the word *encouraging*, so what Dr. Phil had said did not sound all that bad to me, all in all. So I had a sin-drome. I didn't think I had sinned lately, but maybe I had done a sin and didn't even know it. There are so many sins to remember not to do, and every week at church, the preacher added new ones.

Our preacher always said sin gives you a black heart, yet I couldn't recall him ever saying anything about sin turning you a different color on the outside, just the inside. But I figured that if my heart could turn black, then maybe my outside could too. Our preacher said people fall into sin, but he never told us where they fell from. He did say if you fell into a sin, you needn't worry because you wouldn't fall from grace if you'd never been in grace to begin with. I didn't know where God stored grace. As a matter of fact, I didn't recall falling from anywhere at all—from sin or grace or anywhere else. But I did decide that I'd better think seriously about which sin I might have done to cause such a sin-drome. I tried my best, but couldn't remember anything bad that I had done lately.

I finally figured that if it wasn't sin turning me a different color, then it must have something to do with the weather in the South—maybe if you lived in South Carolina, sooner or later, your skin turned black. Our teacher at school had told us once that 72 percent of the people in Beaufort County were black.

When I asked Mama if you turned black because you lived in the South or because you had done a sin, she said that was the worst thing she had ever heard me say. She said it was unfortunate that sin had been described as having a color at all, because if anything, its color should have been bright red since it was more like fire. Sin burned people.

"And as long as I'm talking about colors," she said, "everyone in the world has pink hearts. They aren't black. Period."

She was almost yelling at me. I was stunned. She had never yelled at me before—only at Scooter. Scooter got yelled at all the time. Mama then turned from angry to sad and said, "I am terribly disappointed in you for thinking something like that, Beebe."

Her eyes got stern, and she added if she ever heard me say anything like that again, she would tan my hide, which confused me. I certainly didn't want my hide to turn tan. One color change was enough for me. I was still getting used to being purple. I looked like a big grape. It didn't help that Mama was now upset with me, and my daddy wasn't home to comfort me—he was gone to Puerto Rico. We had plenty of air that you could fly in above Beaufort, but the Marines liked the air better closer to Cuba, for some reason.

In the end, the worst part of the sin-drome was the part that left Mama disappointed in me because of what I had said. That was not a good feeling. It left me feeling awful inside. I was glad Daddy wasn't home because he might have been disappointed in me also, and that would have been too much to bear. I turned over in my hospital bed and tried not to cry. People always want to know what the matter is when you start to cry, and sometimes you just can't explain.

Mama reached over and touched me on the ear. "Oh, Beebe. I'm sorry. I'm so sorry. I'm just so sick of the attitudes of some people about other people. We'll talk more about this when you are well. I don't know what came over me. Hush now. I love you with my whole heart, and that's the truth. I know you didn't mean what you said the way it came out. I was just so worried about you that I lost control of myself, and I'm disappointed that I raised my voice. Will you forgive me?"

My heart swelled. It sure felt better not to be the only one who was disappointed in herself. Maybe there was hope for me yet.

"You didn't sin, Beebe, and you didn't change colors because you did something wrong. You are bruised over every inch of your body because you are very, very sick. God doesn't make us sick. He is a healer, and we are going to ask him to heal you right now."

And we did.

My mother prayed for everything—big and little—all the time, so asking God to heal me wasn't out of the ordinary for her at all. She was on one-to-one speaking terms with Jesus and his dad. She must have outdone herself praying for me to get well that night because I started to get better soon after that, and I overheard the nurses say it was a miracle.

CHAPTER 18

GRADUALLY I RETURNED TO MY original color. Not all at once nor overnight, but every day you could see my skin lighten a bit more.

"Dr. Phil, is my heart really pink?"

"Yes, of course! All hearts are pink. Practically everything under everybody's skin is pink."

What a relief! However, since I couldn't see my heart, I kept my sins 'fessed up from then on just in case the preacher was right about sin turning your heart black.

"You've made me famous, Rebecca!" Dr. Phil told me. "Because you got well from such a dreadful disease, everyone thinks I saved your life. I didn't tell them it was probably because your mama was praying to Jesus for you. Everybody thinks I saved the day, and, well, it's kinda nice being a hero for a change."

I knew Dr. Phil had been at the hospital every day for the entire two weeks that I was dying and not dying and changing colors. I had heard him barking orders to everyone in the place and making sure that I had ice cream and anything else I wanted any time I wanted it. Mama said Dr. Phil saved my life, but that prayers always help. Personally, I think

God knew what Dr. Phil was doing for me and helped him out. Our preacher told us that God likes Jews almost as much as he likes Baptists. Given that God's son, Jesus, was a Jew, that always made sense to me.

My daddy never got to see me when I changed colors. Mama begged the Marines to let him come in from the field, but the Marines said no. They needed him. He was the only one who had experience constructing a tarmac landing strip in rough terrain—since he had helped build one in Spain. "We have to keep him here," the group commander said. "It's critical. Our boys are dying in Vietnam. We have to lay an airfield near Chu Lai, and we've got to see how quick we can get this process down. Every day counts. He has to help us with it. We don't have anyone else around here who has done this before."

"I don't have anyone else either," my mama told him. "This is his little girl, and she might not make it. If he is going to see her alive again he has to come in now."

"No," the colonel said, "I'm sorry, ma'am, but time is critical. More lives than your daughter's life depend on it. I know that doesn't make it any better, but he has to help us now. Not later. It can't wait."

"Neither can she," Mama told him.

The commander was probably a good man, but he was a Marine, and Marines don't think quite like mothers do.

I didn't die.

That was good because I sure didn't want them to stick me in a hole in South Carolina. No one would ever find me there when it was time to head for Beulah Land. I don't know where that is, but the preacher talks about Beulah Land all the time. He says that when our days on earth are over and the resurrection comes, we'll all go together to Beulah Land. If he's right, I want to make sure someone knows where I am when the time comes.

CHAPTER 19

Pryor, Oklahoma
2010

"LUNCH IS READY," MY MOTHER called to me from downstairs. "I'm out on the patio. Are you ready to eat?" "Coming—" I hollered back. I wasn't getting anything done anyway. I had been sidetracked by my past.

We sat down to a lunch of chicken-pecan sandwiches that Mama had made. The crust had been neatly trimmed and relegated to the big green plastic bowl that held bread crumbs until it was time for Mama to make bread pudding, meat loaf, or stuffing. "For later," she would always say as she trimmed away the crusts. "I don't want to waste good bread." And of course, the bowl had its own special place in the cabinet over the double oven. "Warm air drifts up there when I bake. Dries the crumbs quicker." My mother had a reason for everything she did.

The sandwiches were cut diagonally, each side an exact mirror of the other, and she had used an ice cream scoop to place a perfect mound of potato salad on a lettuce leaf on the side—complete with a green olive on top, pimento side up, perpendicular to the surface of the potato salad. A napkin was folded precisely Japanese style, like an origami kite, and placed on the right of the plate. Just so. Mama was the neatest, most exacting person God ever made. She was still standing when she took the first bite of her sandwich and asked what I thought. "Does it need pickles?"

I declared the sandwich perfect. She seemed satisfied and sat down and opened a bag of chips. "Have I forgotten anything?" she asked as she picked up her napkin, folded it precisely around half of her sandwich, and waited for an answer.

"Nope," I said. "Let's eat."

We bowed our heads and Mama gave the blessing.

It was one of those clear, crisp Oklahoma September days. Rain the night before had left the foliage so clean you could see the veins in each leaf from where we sat on the sunporch.

The foliage had not yet started to turn, and the leaves were waxed with a silvery shine from the rain. The first frost was still six or seven weeks away. Oklahoma was in the last days of Indian summer . . . those last few weeks when you knew summer was almost over, but the gardens were still producing fruit and vegetables in abundance and the petunias and begonias were in full bloom.

Chrysanthemums filled the flower beds—lavender, yellow, and burnt-orange buds beginning to open. Crape myrtle rose on gnarled trunks the size of your arm, edging the serpentine brick path that led to the backyard shed. White, fuchsia, and pink blooms burst from the top of the crape myrtle like thick frosting on a birthday cake. Perfectly spaced, the bushes marched toward the potting shed where the garden tools were stored.

Of course, Mama's entire backyard was carefully planned and placed to please the eye, flowers and shrubs organized by the month they would bloom. Every season had its own color, March through October. It would have been beyond me to figure all that out, but I found it pleasantly peaceful to sip my tea, eat my sandwich, and admire my mother's perfectly planned garden.

"Mama," I said breaking the silence. "I have a question I've never asked, one I've wondered about from time to time."

"Sure," she said. "Ask away. What do you want to know?"

"Well," I said quietly, hesitantly, "it's about Amy. My little sister. I was wondering what happened to her. You've never said much about it.

All I ever knew was that one day she was here with us and the next day she wasn't."

Mama picked up a potato chip, turned it over and popped it into her mouth. Then, without a word, she proceeded to finish the first half of her sandwich. Finally she stood, threw her napkin away, retrieved another one from the pantry, and wrapped the second half of her sandwich exactly the same way she had wrapped the first half—only then did she speak.

"Well, you and Pat never asked . . . so I never . . . there was no reason. You were only a baby then, and I didn't imagine you would remember; you weren't old enough to remember," she paused. "There's not much to tell. It was so . . ."

I felt like I had chosen the wrong time to ask her. "Forget it," I said. "I was curious. Nobody ever talked about what happened back then, and I got to wondering about her."

"No, we didn't talk about . . . your father and I . . . we didn't want you or Pat to feel our sadness. There didn't seem to be any reason to talk about it. It was done. She was gone. We were broken . . . your father . . . . and I . . . we were in shock for so long. One minute you have a perfect little baby girl, the next minute you don't. How could a person imagine such a thing?"

I knew she didn't expect an answer.

CHAPTER 20

"WHY NOW?" MAMA FINALLY SAID. "What made you think about that today?" "I don't know," I said. "I've been reading my old journal about when we lived in Virginia before the move to Beaufort. I have a fuzzy memory of holding her—Pat and I, in the back seat of a car somewhere, with Amy on a blanket across our laps. The image is like a shadow, more a feeling really. Something we had left behind in Virginia. Have you ever gone back there, back to Virginia?"

"Back to Virginia? Arlington? No. No. We left Virginia and moved to Beaufort, and later, after we moved to Oklahoma, there was no time before your father had to go to . . . and it seemed like . . . well, then I wanted to, but school started for you girls and, of course, Scooter was a full-time job. There was so much to do—helping you children make friends, volunteering at the church, trying to keep my mind busy. Unpacking. Putting everything where it should go. Drapes. The eternal problem of draping windows. No, I never went back. I never went back to Virginia again. It seems like it was yesterday, but . . ."

We watched a flock of hummingbirds dart back and forth about the feeder. "I just counted twenty-three hummingbirds," I said.

"That's sure a lot of hummingbirds for September," Mama said. "I've been seeing more of them since I switched to a red sugar-water feeder. They always say hummingbirds are attracted to red."

We sat in comfortable silence, watching the activity at the feeder.

"You probably wouldn't remember," Mama said. "You weren't yet three years old when we found a better house and moved closer to base—two weeks before Amy was born. I painted the entire house the week we moved in. Closer to base, always looking for something closer to base. I was eight-and-a-half months pregnant, so huge that I could hardly stretch to reach the ceilings to paint them. By the grace of God, I didn't fall off the ladder. I had to do the painting by myself because your father was deep into junior school and couldn't take a break.

"That's an unfinished piece of my life. I was so thankful that I hadn't lost either one of you two girls, and I felt so guilty that such a thought would cross my mind. Being thankful that you two were alive seemed a betrayal of her, of Amy. Like somehow I was choosing in my mind which one of you I would rather keep or which one for God to take."

I reached out and touched her shoulder. "Oh, Mama. You didn't choose. You had no choice! God isn't like that!"

"I know that—in my head. In my heart, well, I was just glad you and Pat were alive and . . . yet at the same time, I was devastated that Amy wasn't. I was only twenty-three years old—three babies in five years, seven moves, grief-stricken, trying to be what everyone, especially your father, needed. I was learning how to do all that on the fly. "Her being gone. That was beyond my ability to fathom, to comprehend. I didn't seem to be able to work it all out in my own mind. The loss. And I didn't have anyone to talk to, no one to help me figure out how such a thing could happen to us. What was God thinking? What was the reason? What had I done wrong; maybe I shouldn't have painted the house—could it have been the paint fumes? Maybe the move closer to base, carrying all those boxes? A million times I asked myself, *why, why, why?* She was perfect. Nine days later, she quit breathing.

"And then, well, then our lives went on. They had to go on. Your father was halfway through junior school at Quantico. He had to finish, and I had you and Pat to worry about. Who could possibly explain to people how we lived through the loss? Much less what it was like to be military people at such a time.

"What happened was just one more unexplainable crisis in our lives, with not enough time to figure it out before the next crisis arrived. In a way, ignoring the cascade of emotions seemed normal to me. That's what military spouses do—we just keep on keeping on. You would drown in emotions if you stopped to think about how tragic it all was. So I just didn't talk about it. To anyone."

Mama fell quiet for a moment before looking over at me as if to ask if I had an answer to this unfathomable question.

"Our lives were chaotic. Fighter pilots operating off carriers in every ocean. The Atlantic. The Pacific. The Gulf. So we moved. Again and again. We endured; we moved; we kept on going. I guess I put all of that on a shelf to think about later, and then never seemed to find a moment to do that in the years that followed."

I didn't speak. What could I say? That the years had become decades? Instead, I sat there. Silent. I could tell she wasn't through, just regrouping.

CHAPTER 21

"YOUR FATHER COULD NOT take time off from school because we had had a tragedy. He had to keep going too. He had made Major, so at least we had a little extra money and were able to buy another car. Pat started kindergarten, and you and I were left at home, just the two of us. We'd drive to the Smithsonian or to a junk store or to the zoo—anywhere, just to get us out of the house. I hadn't unpacked much of anything before I went into labor with Amy, only the necessities. Sheets, a few pots and dishes. I'd been too busy painting the house and getting ready to bring the baby home. The hard part was what to do with all the baby things and the empty crib. I didn't want to deal with them."

"I remember helping you fold baby clothes. I thought you had bought them for our dolls," I told her.

"Well, you did get a Chatty Cathy for your birthday that year, so I can see why you might have thought that," she said. "I finally got everything put away. Weeks went by, then months, a year. I was in limbo. I couldn't seem to get started again with anything. I would wash the clothes, forget to hang them out, and find them soured in the washing machine a few days later. Or I'd hang them out and forget to bring them in before they got dirty hanging on the line—or soaked in the rain. I alternated between shutdown and going in circles. And then before I could even get my thoughts around what had happened to us, I was pregnant with Scott."

A quiet engulfed us until I broke it, saying "I remember one thing clearly, and that's how much I loved those days we spent together—just you and me. Pat was in school. I had you all to myself; I had never been an only child before. I had no idea what your life was like at the time, only that mine was so happy and how wonderful it was to get up every day and go *looking* with you. 'Let's go *looking*, Beebe,' you would say. And we did. We'd get dressed, eat breakfast, take Pat to kindergarten, and off we would go.

"Every day was an adventure, Mama."

"Then I guess something good happened that year, and I did enjoy that part too. I remember you and me and going looking. I remember Pat and taking her to kindergarten, telling her to have a happy day, which she never did. Another regret from that time is what your sister suffered during those months while I was in a fog."

"What are you talking about, Mama. Why do you say she suffered?"

"Pat's kindergarten teacher was awful, and I didn't even notice that anything was wrong. Maybe if I had been paying more attention, it could have been avoided. The teacher had been putting Pat in a closet three or four times a week—all by herself—and shutting the closet door on her. I only learned what was going on when one of the other mothers told me. Pat never said a word about it. They fired the teacher, but it was too late for Pat. She suffered through it. Silently. You know how she is. Stoic. She's always done what she had to do to get through things. Put one foot in front of the other like your dad does."

"She never said a word to me!" I said.

"No, she wouldn't," Mama said. "She didn't tell anyone. Not even her own mother. I blame myself—I should have waited another year to put her in kindergarten, but when you tested like she tested, well, they said it was best for a child like that to start school. She didn't turn five until the week after school began. She was too young, no matter what the experts said, and I was too young to know how old a child should

74

be emotionally before they started school. I should have held her more too. Maybe then she would have told me what the teacher was doing."

"What do you mean, Mama? You held us! We were always in your lap—reading a book, rocking, singing songs."

"Not after Amy," she said. "And a year later when Scott was just a week old, your dad received orders to report to Beaufort. Those eternal 'orders.' Three weeks later, we left Virginia for South Carolina. We moved again. Your dad was ecstatic because he was done with school and going back to flying; he had orders to a squadron. But for me, it was just another move. I was twenty-five years old and had already lived a lifetime." A little smile appeared on her face. "That thing you said you remembered—about holding her, holding Amy—we were on our way home from car hunting in Washington, D.C. We needed a second car even though we could barely afford another. You and Pat kept asking me if you could hold her and I kept saying no, that she was too little. Finally, your father said, 'Why don't you let them have her? You'll be careful, won't you, girls?'

"I'm so glad I listened to him. That picture of you three together is a memory I pull out every now and then. Three little girls. I once had three little girls. You held her so gently . . . like she was a tiny angel, which she probably was. An angel. Amy accomplished exactly what God sent her to do. I think perhaps your father and I needed to learn some things, but it was years before I understood that—that she had had a complete, full life in nine days."

Mama's voice trailed off. "Why don't we go inside where it's cooler?" she suggested. "I'll get you a fresh cup of tea."

I followed her into the kitchen. Mama put the kettle back on the burner and took out two tea bags from the cupboard. A few minutes later, she set the steaming cups on the round oak coffee table, the same table our neighbor had cut the legs down on so many years before. We drank our tea and made small talk.

After a spell, Mama said, "She looked like Patty. Blue eyes and quiet, very quiet. She was a good baby. Pretty. Very pretty. She was perfect. She was so sweet and we all loved her instantly. A perfect little girl.

"My perfect little girl."

CHAPTER 22

A FTER TEA, I RETURNED TO MY OLD room and began to tackle the last drawer in the dresser. I set aside a stack of *Seventeen* magazines to deal with later and fished out a bottom-of-the-drawer smattering of paper clips, rubber bands, and crumpled pieces of paper. All of it headed to the trash. Underneath, a yellowed note caught my eye. It was addressed to my mother.

> *Rebecca seems to have a problem telling the truth. She says her sister is buried at Arlington. We both know that isn't true, and I think you need to address the problem. Lying is a serious offense, and lies of this nature are an insult to our great General Robert E. Lee.*

My mind returned to that day in first grade when the teacher ordered me to write over and over again on the blackboard:

My sister is not buried at Arlington.
My sister is not buried at Arlington.
My sister is not buried at Arlington.

I remembered waiting until the teacher left the room to quickly scrawl on the board:

She is too

. . . before I slipped out the side door and ran home.

Why didn't I get into trouble for my insurrection at school? Had Mama spoken to my teacher and straightened her out? I remembered how I had dreaded returning to school the next day, knowing the teacher would be angry with me about what I had written on the board. And how surprised I was when the teacher said nothing about it at all. Now I knew why. After Pat's kindergarten experience, Mama had promised herself never to let a teacher bully one of her children again. Mama must have intervened with the teacher on my behalf.

I finished going through my old *Seventeen* magazines, stacked them to the side to dispose of later, and decided to take a nap. By the time I woke up from it, Mama was in the kitchen starting supper. I took a shower, carried the pile of magazines and trash bags out to the garbage, and then joined her.

"Need any help?" I asked. "Would you like me to peel the potatoes?"

"No, it's under control. I just need to fix these green beans."

As she reached for the beans, she whispered, "I didn't want her, you know. I had just spent nine months in misery pregnant. I did not want another baby after that, after spending a year caring for two babies in diapers by myself. Had I known I was pregnant with *Amy*, I would have been fine, but I didn't know I loved her until I held her in my arms. I loved her. She was my child. I loved her, but it was too late to tell her. I felt it had to be my fault because I hadn't wanted another baby. I couldn't help but think that maybe God was punishing me . . . for my attitude about being pregnant again."

Her chin started to tremble, and tears began to slip down her checks.

I couldn't have been more shocked. My mother never cried. She never fell apart. No matter what, she pulled herself together and kept on keeping on. That was the constant that ran through my life, that grounded me despite all the moves, all the new schools.

"Something worse is happening to someone, somewhere, today," Mama would always say. "Our current circumstances are made bearable in comparison. We can get through this."

And we did.

We always did.

However, I knew that the military could take a toll on wives. Many marriages didn't survive the military much less the death of a child.

Mama wiped her face with a hand towel and took off her apron—the beans forgotten. She reached for a napkin she didn't need, and began to fold it lengthwise over and over into the shape of a thin straw. Then she slowly and methodically twisted the napkin into a long, tight candy cane. She was so neat about everything she did. Orderly—even about grief. Finally, she untwisted the napkin and placed it on the dining table to the left of her sterling-silver fork. Perfectly parallel. I couldn't help wondering if millions of twisted napkins were lined up in a drawer somewhere waiting to be untwisted and used. Without another word, she stepped back to the green beans and put them on the stove to cook, and then moved outside to the porch swing, seemingly lost in thought.

Mama appeared done with talking, to my relief. I checked the water level in the pan of green beans, turned the burner to low, fixed two glasses of iced tea, and joined her on the back porch. "You've done a fantastic job arranging things back here, Mama. Your garden is beautiful. Why don't you show me what you've done lately?"

Tea glasses in hand, we wandered through the garden as Mama pointed out her new ever-blooming hydrangeas and the pink lilies she had repositioned along the edge of the vegetable garden. "The lilies started to bloom yesterday," she said. "That's always such a surprise. The leaves come up in the spring only to die back and vanish. Then in August, when everything else is burned up, stalks shoot up out of the ground overnight with big pink blooms. No wonder folks call them surprise lilies."

We had been making small talk for awhile when she suddenly said, "After we moved to Beaufort, I should have arranged for someone to take flowers to Amy, but I didn't know anyone in Virginia very well—not anyone I could ask to put flowers . . ."

In that moment, I regretted ever asking about my sister. I tried to change the subject. "Since we're talking about flowers," I said, "why don't we pick some of those pink lilies over there for the table?"

Mama nodded, and afterward, we wandered back into the house with our arms full of lilies. I looked for a vase while Mama, still holding lilies in her arms, settled herself on one of the love seats, only to stand, sit back down, and then return to her story as if compelled. Years and years—decades in fact—had passed since Amy went to Arlington, but it might as well have been yesterday. Why had Mama never talked to any of us before about losing Amy? Why had she held it in for so long? Then again, I had never lost a child. What did I know about such a loss?

"It wasn't just the flowers," Mama suddenly said. "Every time we moved . . . and every place we left behind . . . everything in my life seemed . . . always unfinished, like I had left pieces of myself scattered across the country. But when we left Virginia, I left her behind. I left Amy. That has always felt wrong."

She stopped and looked at me. "Maybe I should go back there to see if I can find the place where she is."

I could almost see the wheels turning in her head as if she were doing the mental calculations that would be involved in getting from Oklahoma back to Virginia—how she would travel, how many days it would take—lining up the sequence of events in an orderly manner in her mind. That's what Mama always did when an idea occurred to her. She figured it all out and put it in order. First, second, third—one step after another—until she had it organized like she had envisioned it. I had never been able to do that. I always jumped in, started in the middle, and then muddled my way out in all directions. Not Mama. I could see the idea of returning to Virginia take hold in her mind.

"You know, Mama, that's a wonderful idea," I said. "The trip might be a nice break after we get all of this stuff cleared out of the house. Before you move. Correction, if you move. I'll go with you if you like."

"Oh, that would be nice!" Mama said. "It would take at least two, probably three days to make the drive. I'm no longer a spring chicken. No way we could drive eight hundred miles in a day again. But then, I doubt you remember the last time we did that. Back when your dad's folks asked us to visit them in northern California. They wanted to get to know you two girls. You were eight months old. Pat was two. Babies, both of you.

"At the time, we were staying with my family in Oklahoma while your dad was off somewhere—Japan, I think it was, for thirteen months. Before your father had left, he had qualified a squadron of F4Ds to land on the carrier. It was a horribly dangerous airplane called the Skyray. And the effort had gone poorly. So many had crashed in training that they called the shore off El Toro: Skyray Bay. I remember one of the pilots ignored instructions, hit the carrier, and pulled out the fuel line. He refused to eject and was killed. Another pilot broke his back crashing into the carrier ramp. Deckhands destroyed two other airplanes—all in the two weeks before your father left to go overseas. I didn't see how they'd all survive another year flying that plane.

"I figured we would be better off in Oklahoma with my folks, and your father agreed. But your father's folks wanted us to come stay with them for a while, so I drove us from Oklahoma to California. We arrived at two in the morning, having traveled eight hundred miles two days in a row. Where did I ever get the nerve to do that? I was only in my early twenties at the time."

Mama looked down at the lilies still in her arms and said, "I could get some roses for Amy. Pink? Pink roses?"

"We can fly," I said. "No need to spend two days on the road."

"No. I don't fly."

"It's safer than driving."

"No."

"Well, you can think about how to get there later—after you get this house the way you want it. Plenty of time to make a plan," I said. "Later, when you don't have so much to do."

"I'm *not* flying."

CHAPTER 23

DADDY FINALLY GOT TO COME home from where he had been laying tarmac after I had my sin-drome. He couldn't seem to decide whether to squeeze me to death or shake Dr. Phil's hand off in gratitude. "Thank you, Doc, for my little girl," he said. "I'll never be able to repay you."

Dr. Phil looked at me and winked. "Well, I needed someone to read the newspaper to me," he said. "Andy can't read—and someone has to hold the paper so I can concentrate on tying my knots."

Everyone seemed happy to have me safely home from the hospital. Jeanette even supplied Andy and me with Coca-Cola, a treat usually off-limits at my house.

"A few *coki-coulars* won't hurt her," Jeanette told my mother in her northern twang.

"Well," my mother said, "maybe one or two won't ruin her teeth."

Every day from then on, Andy and I drank Coca-Cola at his house. Andy's mom must have thought my mother meant one or two colas *every day* instead of one or two *period.* I wasn't going to be the one to straighten her out. Mama never bought cola, chips, or any other kind of junk food. "Bad for your teeth," she always told us.

The very next month, my daddy repaid the debt to Dr. Phil for saving my life. You don't often get to do that in the Marine Corps; you usually just help the next guy. And if you're always helping somebody with something, then anyone who needs some help gets help, which is usually the next family that moves onto your street. Most of the time, you don't even know who the newcomers are. Someone goes over and invites their kids to come play; someone else takes over food and a coffeepot; and another family helps them unpack and hang drapes. Every woman on the base has a box of drapes that won't work after they change houses, so drapes are passed around. Mama says that when your drape boxes take up half of the moving van, you get to retire from the military.

The night I came home from the hospital was a homemade-ice-cream night. Neighbors brought cookies and freezers full of peach and peppermint ice cream over to our house along with their lawn chairs, which they set up in our backyard, where Mama had a big tank of coffee and such on a table. We were Baptists, so we didn't drink or serve alcohol—only coffee or tea with tons of ice and sugar.

Sometimes we had big dinners on the lawn. Everybody brought their kids and a covered dish, and then stayed until sundown swapping stories, playing games, and listening to the tree frogs chirruping in the live oaks across the street. Deeper in the woods, the bullfrogs harrumphed and owls hooted. The chirruping, harrumphing, and hooting were the background chorus to our evening gatherings, a Laurel Bay symphony.

Ours was the last house at the end of the block, on the corner where the road turned back toward the bay and the woods began. Our street was a wonderfully exciting place in the day, and a wonderfully scary place at night. After the sun went down, the woods would turn into a more sinister, eerie place with their long ghost arms of Spanish moss dangling from the limbs of the oaks, swaying in the dark.

The occasional whine of jets coming in overhead was the only man-made noise that broke the summer sounds, but even the frogs had become accustomed to the constant roar of the jet engines and picked their songs right back up again after the planes had passed over. The

roar of the jets was such a constant backdrop to our lives, no one seemed
to notice, not even the ghosts. The adults would stop mid-sentence,
wait for the jets to pass, then pick up the sentence on the next word.
They also took turns yelling, "Don't go too far in those woods and get
lost!" That was an unnecessary warning because none of us kids was
that brave. We had seen the snakes that lived under the rotting logs and
the spiders that scurried from beneath, and so none of us was about to
venture too deep into the woods at night.

When playing ghost games became too scary, one of us would yell,
"Let's go back and get some more ice cream!" No one ever wanted to be
the one who yelled first and got labeled a chicken, so we waited as long
as we could stand it—hoping someone else would yell first. When they
did, back to the party we went.

The evening of my return, we came in from the shadows and found
Dr. Phil and my dad in a deep discussion over bowls of peach ice cream.

"Sure, I'll take you," I heard my father say, "but you have to go
through the pressure chamber first. That's a requirement. You have to
know what anoxia feels like."

"You'd do that for me?" Dr. Phil said.

He looked dumbfounded.

Dr. Phil never looked dumbfounded.

"If there's something I can do to help you, Phil, I am glad to do
it. It's no big deal; I'd do it for anybody. I need some nighttime hours
anyway, so you'll be helping me out. But you have to go through the
pressure chamber first, and then, well, after you do that, you have to do
one other thing before we can go. Let me know when you finish the
pressure chamber, and we'll talk about what comes next."

"What's the other thing?"

"Why don't you wait until you finish the pressure chamber first.
After that, you might not even want to go," my father said.

Dr. Phil looked doubtful.

"For the anoxia they put you inside the chamber, seal the door, and
remove the oxygen until you pass out. Most people don't like it because
you get light-headed before you faint. You do it so that if you're in an
airplane, lose oxygen, and start to black out, you'll recognize you need

to take some action, check your oxygen, and get to a lower altitude. Hey, it's a safety precaution."

"I know what anoxia is," Dr. Phil said. "I've been on duty at the hospital for chamber trials. I've seen people go through it. No problem, I'll go through the pressure chamber. So tell me the second thing. But now. Not later."

"Well, okay, Phil . . . but you aren't going to like this part. You have to do a trial run on the ejection seat. And as I recall, you once said that only an idiot would get into a plane that had an ejection seat. Anyway, they give you a test-fire so you'll know what to do and how to fire it. Not that you'll ever need it, but it is a requirement. If you're serious, do those two things, and I'll take you. Let me know when you've finished the tests."

Andy and I said together, "Take him where?"

"Philadelphia. Your dad is going to fly me to Philadelphia," Dr. Phil said. "I have an interview for a job, a dream job, and we're so broke and far in debt that I was going to turn it down. No money for a plane ticket. Who around here would volunteer to give up his weekend to take me, a Golfeder, to Philadelphia? I think I'm the only Jew on this base, and if you haven't noticed, we're not that popular down here in the South."

He turned to my dad. "Thanks. Thank you. I don't know what to say."

"It's no big deal, Phil. Forget it. You're my friend. And I would fly you somewhere for the rest of the weekends I've got left in my life. A million weekend hops couldn't repay . . . anyway, last I heard, that's what friends do. I'd do the same thing for any friend. Besides, I need the nighttime hours; I'm behind."

I could tell my daddy was embarrassed. If there was something he couldn't stand, it was a compliment. No one said a word about him having flown every night that week either. He certainly didn't need more nighttime hours. Dr. Phil would have known that anyway—he lived right next-door and worked almost as many nights in the emergency room as my father did at the squadron. Sometimes they waved at each other as they passed on their way home from an all-nighter on base.

86

"How come you're going to fly with my dad?" I asked Dr. Phil the next day as we were reading the newspaper on his porch. "You told me and Andy that a person would have to be nuts to get in an airplane that needed an ejection seat."

"I must have been pulling your leg if I told you that," Dr. Phil said.

"No, you weren't teasing me. You said a guy would have to be certifiably nuts to fly in an A-4. That's what you said!"

"Well, Rebecca, I was wrong. First time for everything."

"So you're really going to fly with my dad?"

"You and Andy go get the paper. Let's talk about something else. Something that doesn't involve being certifiably nuts."

CHAPTER 24

SOME NIGHTS DR. PHIL and my father would sit in our living room, drinking iced tea and playing cribbage while Scooter, Pat, Andy, and I played Monopoly. Pat always won our games, but as the summer passed, I got better. The challenge of the game was to keep Scooter from throwing the little red hotels up in the air and catching them in his mouth as they fell—while keeping Andy from picking up the ones that made it to the carpet and eating them. Pat and I decided it was a boy thing.

Daddy and Dr. Phil were evenly matched at cribbage but different in every other way. My father was blue-eyed, blond, and built like a block of concrete. Dr. Phil, as I told you, with his small stature and curly black hair could have been a gnome. The two of them spent hours debating the merits of the Marine Corps versus the Navy as well as a dozen other subjects. Neither of them ever seemed to win their debates, but I could tell they both enjoyed the battle.

"Stimulating," my father said. "I like a man who can think and present his opinions with conviction."

"But, Daddy, you don't agree with each other most of the time," I reminded him.

"Doesn't matter. We both know what we believe. Best way to learn something new is in a friendly debate with the opposition. You have to respect a man who has thought out his position with intelligence and can defend it with dignity."

I think one reason my father said that was because he and Dr. Phil had been known to discuss religion. My family liked Moses and Jehovah okay, but we weren't as attached to them as Dr. Phil was. We liked Jesus and his daddy better. I think Jesus's daddy was once called Jehovah, but then he must have been given another name too, because the Baptists always call him "Our Dear Heavenly Father."

One good thing was that the Ten Commandments worked just fine for all of us.

CHAPTER 25

DR. PHIL DIDN'T HAVE A SOUL. He wasn't the only one. A whole bunch of men on our street in Beaufort didn't have a soul. I don't know about the women on our street, but all of the children on our block still had theirs. I know because I asked our preacher. He said all of us kids still had our souls because we weren't accountable just yet. You had to reach a certain age to be accountable, he told me.

Our preacher talked about lost souls all the time. He said that losing your soul wasn't your fault; it was Adam's fault. He assured us that children were safe until they knew that they weren't. But after that, they were accountable. The way the preacher explained it was that everybody who had lost their soul used to have a soul—back when they were a little kid—before they got accountable and lost it.

It was all very confusing.

I don't know what Adam ever did to make our preacher so upset, but Adam sure messed things up for everyone else. And the way I looked at it, with all the people in our neighborhood who had lost or sold their souls, you couldn't be too careful. Dr. Phil had lost his soul because he sold it to the Navy to go to medical school. Another man on our block sold his soul to go to law school, and one man on the next block sold his soul to go to dental school—Daddy told me that. Anyway, Dr. Phil didn't have his soul anymore. He had sold it. That made me sad. I asked my daddy if he still had his soul or if he had sold his to somebody too.

"No, I've still got mine," Daddy said. "Don't know anybody who would want the soul of a fighter pilot except the Marine Corps and God himself. You have to be stupid or plumb crazy to fly fighters for the Marines."

I knew my daddy wasn't stupid or crazy because Dr. Phil had told me that my father was smart and very brave. And Dr. Phil would never bear false witness because Moses told all the Jews not to do that, and Dr. Phil had said that was one of the Big Ten.

One night as Daddy pulled into the driveway, I heard Dr. Phil yell from his front porch. "It's done, Ken! Both things. So I'm ready to go. That is, if you still need some nighttime hours."

"You're kidding! I'm surprised. Shocked, I must say," my father replied. "Tell you the truth, Phil, I didn't think you would do it. Well, I guess that officially makes you certifiably nuts like the rest of us, to use your own words. How did you like the ejection-seat trial? Fun, huh?"

"Just promise me I won't ever need to use it!" Dr. Phil hollered.

"Okay, I promise. You won't ever have to use it. If something goes wrong with the plane, I'll fire mine and leave you in the back seat! Do you want to go this weekend?"

"So soon? Don't we need a little time to plan this out?"

"What's to plan? File a flight plan, hop in the plane, fly to Philly, go to your interview, turn around, and fly home. I'll see what kind of two-seater is free, and we'll leave Friday after supper. Seven o'clock, right before dark."

"At night? Two-seater? Don't they have any transports? Something that has two engines, just in case. Shouldn't we go in the daytime when you can see? Couldn't we get something with a couple of propellers? What if the only thing available is something you haven't flown before?

What then? We'll have to wait until you get checked out. Right?" Dr. Phil said.

"Let me see, I don't remember asking you to learn how to use a parachute. Nope, I think it was an ejection seat you qualified for. Not parachutes. So transports are out. Last time I strapped on a parachute was, hmmm, in a Corsair . . . in Korea. That was a lotta years ago. And since I am undoubtedly the world's greatest single-seat jet fighter pilot in the world, shoot, I'm stepping down a peg to fly a two-seater. You want to make me look bad? I'm not flying any transport. No need to embarrass myself."

"Okay, okay, Friday. Ejection seat. Two-seater. I'll be ready. Seven o'clock."

"Good. Glad that's settled. Now get the cribbage board, and we'll see how smart you are and how much smarter I am. Time to take you down a peg or two. I'll peg out before you hit the first turn on the board."

"In a pig's eye," Dr. Phil said.

"You don't like pigs," my daddy reminded him.

"Watch me peg out in a pig's eye," Dr. Phil retorted, "and we'll see who likes pigs."

On Friday night as planned, Daddy and Dr. Phil suited up in bright orange flight suits. Dr. Phil looked like an orange gnome ready to help Linus in the *Peanuts* comic strip welcome the Great Pumpkin into his pumpkin patch.

"I got us an F-80, two seats. No need to worry, I flew the F-80 in the training command in Pensacola—right out of flight school," my daddy told Dr. Phil. "The Navy started the first class in jet aviation; it was brand-new at the time. They picked two of us to go to jet training. The rest of my class graduated and went straight to Korea, and, well, let's just say that their survival rate over there was next to zero. You can't learn enough in flight school to go up against the enemy. The commandant said that no more nuggets were going to war unless they had a year stateside in a squadron. Probably saved my life. Anyway, I learned to fly jets in the F-80. Piece of cake. They renamed the F-80 the TO-2 when they added the second seat and changed the designation from F to T.

Fighter to trainer. We're going to Philly in a trainer. Kind of embarrassing, I'll admit."

"How many years ago did you say that was . . . when you last flew this plane?" Dr. Phil asked.

"Don't think I said. Tell you what, I'll pick up a manual, and you can read it to me on the way to Philly. Give you something to do. And if I've forgotten something, or have a question about anything, I'll just ask you."

"In the dark?" Dr. Phil asked.

"Bring a flashlight. No problem. Take the clothes you need to interview, a toothbrush, and shaving gear. We have zero room in the cockpit, so what we take has to go in the empty gun bay in a soft duffel. You can have all the gun bay for your stuff. All I need is Skivvies, socks, and a toothbrush."

When the big day came, Mama insisted on taking a photograph of the two of them in their orange flight suits before they left. "For posterity," she said. "When you are the world's greatest neurosurgeon, Phil, we can all look back and see how you got there—looking like an orange pumpkin! We'll see you two home tomorrow night."

But they didn't make it home the next night. They got caught in a freak ice storm and had to stay two nights with Dr. Phil's mom and dad in Philadelphia.

"Kosher," Dr. Phil told us later. "My parents are old-world kosher. Matzo balls and gefilte fish. We showed up at their front door still wearing sweaty flight suits, looking like a couple of refugees. Those flight suits must have been hanging in a locker on base since World War II— odoriferous. I thought my mother wasn't going to let us in the house, and since we didn't bring a change of clothes, we had to borrow some of my father's, and he's a lot shorter than either of us. We cleaned up pretty good even though our legs were hanging six inches out of the bottom of our britches. Mom fed us after we took a shower, and the rabbi came over for dinner and declared us clean."

"Mercy, did she feed us!" Daddy said. "You know you've been fed when a Jewish mama gets hold of you. I was so fat by the time we finally left Philly, I wasn't sure I could squeeze back into the cockpit.

Bet I gained five pounds in two days. Phil's mama thought I was the greatest thing since sliced bread—once I took a shower and put on clean clothes—bringing her little boy home 'to get a real job' is how I think she put it."

My daddy was grinning by then and so was Dr. Phil.

Dr. Phil chimed in, "I think my mama wanted to make a Jew out of him, but Ken declined—said he wouldn't look good in a skullcap. Personally, I think it was some of the other rituals that stopped him, such as . . ." Dr. Phil made a snipping motion.

Mama intervened. "Enough, you two. The children are listening."

That's the way it goes in our house. Just when things start to get interesting, someone will say, *Hush, the children are listening!* and send us outside.

"We'll be good," Daddy said and gave Mama a wink. "Phil had his interview, and we suited up to come home—but the weather turned kinda bad, so I decided we better wait."

"Kinda bad!" Phil interrupted, "Ice, sleet, rain, thunder, lightning, gale-force winds. If that's 'kinda bad,' I'd like to know what *really* bad is. And then to top it all off, two days later when the weather cleared, we took off and almost ran out of gas on our return home!"

"We had enough gas," my daddy said. "Or we would have if we hadn't eaten so much at your mama's and weighted the plane down."

Dr. Phil protested. "Ken shut the engine down when the tank was almost empty, and we glided into Beaufort. Lit up to land and did that on fumes."

"I told you everything was fine," my father said. "No problem—practiced it a zillion times and did it for real in Korea a bunch more. Not enough gas to get back after a mission? You just cut the engine. Glide for a few miles. No big deal."

Daddy leaned back and grinned. He was on a roll, as Mama liked say—and even us kids knew that once Daddy got to telling a story, there was no stopping him, so you might as well get comfortable and ready to listen. "I was in an all-weather squadron in Japan a few years ago, and I do mean all weather. Flying the F4D, the Skyray, off a carrier. When you lit the afterburner, it felt like you were in a rocket. We flew the Russian perimeter when nothing else America had at the time could get off the ground—when the weather went to zero visibility, the wind was screaming, and nobody else could fly. Now that, Phil, was *really* bad weather. Scared me, and I'm fearless."

"Let me tell you about fear," Dr. Phil said, motioning for us to pay attention. "When we took off and headed to Philly—Ken flipped the plane sideways, rolled back over, and then climbed straight up. Vertical. I thought I was a dead man. Crazy Marine jet jockey. Hardest thing I've ever done was to get back in that plane when we had to come home. Though to be fair, I guess now that we're back home safe and alive, the truth is, I'd never been in an airplane before . . . any kind of airplane."

"What? You never told me that!" my daddy said. "I can't believe you never flew before. Good grief, Phil! Why didn't you say something?"

Dr. Phil's face broke into a big smile. "I was worried you wouldn't take me if I told you I'd never flown and that I am terrified of flying."

"Well, you're right!" my daddy retorted. "At the least, I would have given it a bit more thought. Talk about being certifiably nuts. I still can't believe you did the ejection-seat training. Gee, Phil. You're a much braver man than I thought. Nuts, but brave. Still, you should have told me."

"Probably," Dr. Phil said, "but what an experience! Once in a life-time. How many guys get to fly with a Marine pilot in a fighter jet? I wouldn't take a million dollars for the experience, and I won't ever do it again. And that's a promise!"

Two weeks later Dr. Phil came over after supper with a letter in his hand. "I got the job." He was grinning. "Next year, we're going to Philly. In a car. Or a train. Or a bus. No more airplanes for me."

"This calls for a celebration," my mother said. "We'll make peach ice cream tonight. Ask Jeanette if she will bake some cookies."

"Are you going to get your soul back when you get out of the Navy and get your new job?" I asked Dr. Phil. "Or does the Navy keep it?"

"You betcha! I'm gonna get it back, Rebecca, and I'm taking it with me to Philadelphia. And I promise you I'm not going to sell it to any-body ever again."

I was glad to hear that. Everybody needs a soul. I was also sad. Dr. Phil, the one person on the planet who treated me as if I had a brain, was leaving. Just when I thought everything was perfect. Just when we were all so happy. But that's life in the military. You made friends, and then they left. Or you left.

Friends were always leaving.

Coming and going.

But a year was a long time away.

I'd think about the Golfeders leaving some other time.

CHAPTER 26

A FEW WEEKS AFTER Dr. Phil and Daddy returned from Philly, Dr. Phil ordered the Philadelphia newspaper, and I started to find out about some things that I was pretty sure only a few people down here in Beaufort knew about. Dr. Phil, Andy, and I would read the Philadelphia paper every evening at five thirty. Andy liked the comics, and I liked that the paper had stories from around the world. Reading that newspaper was a lot better than going to first grade. Nothing ever happened at school that I didn't already know. I just endured it and lived for recess, lunch, and the dismissal bell.

Reading the Philadelphia newspaper was the start of me learning about stuff—stuff like a war that was going on in Vietnam. Marines were fighting something they called *gooks* over there, and fighter pilots were being shot down in the jungle and some of them were being captured as prisoners of war. "Dr. Phil, why are they fighting a war? What does it mean that Marines are being sent there?" I asked. "Why do they take pilots for prisoners? Where is Vietnam? What's a *gook*? Why hasn't anyone told me about all this stuff before now?"

Dr. Phil opened his mouth to speak, but nothing came out. He folded up the newspaper, stuck his string in his pocket, and before he could answer me, I said, "And another thing—what pilots are they talking about?"

Dr. Phil took a deep breath and said, "Let's go in the kitchen and get Andy's mother to fix us all a Coke float."

I followed him as asked. When you can't get an answer one place, I've learned that you just have to go find it in another.

"Where in the world did you hear such a word?" my father asked.

"In the Philadelphia newspaper," I said. "It said some Marine came home to Philadelphia and that he never wanted to see another gook as long as he lived and breathed."

"Where did you get a Philadelphia newspaper?"

"Dr. Phil."

"Oh, Phil gets the Philadelphia paper now?"

"Yep, he says it's a *real* newspaper."

"Well, your mother is better with words than I am. Go ask her."

Mama stepped out of the kitchen and gave my daddy the look. "Beebe," she said, "do you remember when I told you that there are some unkind words that you should never say? That word is another one you can add to the list."

Daddy then refreshed my memory by repeating all the others on the list. "Those are the ones we don't ever use," he told me.

Mama gave him the look again. "*Ever!*" she said.

When Daddy saw the look on Mama's face, he added, "I'm saying them out loud so she will be sure to know what the bad ones are."

Despite Daddy's protest of innocence, it looked to me as if he might very well be in trouble with Mama again. "Those are words that some people use to make someone else feel bad," Mama said, "or to make them feel unimportant. They hurt. We don't use words like that in this family. And if someone else uses such words at school, you have to tell them that it's wrong to call people those kinds of names." My mother had pretty strong feelings on the subject of unkind behavior. More than once, I had heard her explain to someone, *Jesus said there weren't going to be any Jews or Gentiles, slaves or masters, males or females. So it doesn't matter if you are red, yellow, black, or white. We are all God's children, and we don't call each other names. Ever.*

Mama turned and gave me the look. "Ever."

Then she turned back to Daddy and said, "*Ever.*"

"Got it!" Daddy said, looking contrite.

Done reminding me about what the Bible has to say about every-one being equal in the eyes of God, Mama sent me outside to play. I still didn't know what a *gook* was, but I was smart enough to know it couldn't be good. I hadn't gotten to ask either of them about wars or Vietnam. Maybe I didn't want to know. I'd seen stories about Vietnam in the Philadelphia newspaper; that was probably somewhere people from Philadelphia went.

My parents had never said anything about a Vietnam. The Beaufort paper never said anything about Vietnam either. And so far, from what I had read in Dr. Golfeder's newspaper from Philly, Vietnam did not sound like a place I wanted to hear more about anyway. No one in Laurel Bay had ever mentioned gooks at school, or the Vietnam War, for that matter. They did talk plenty about the Civil War—despite that being like a hundred years ago.

I'd be grown before they ever got to Vietnam.

CHAPTER 27

I PASSED FIRST GRADE WITH ease and exited not having learned a single thing that mattered. The whole school effort had been a waste of my time, as far as I was concerned, but now I had a three-month reprieve before second grade started.

Summer vacation in Beaufort meant that kids were everywhere, hollering and climbing trees, slamming doors and drinking Kool-Aid. I was perfectly happy, but Mama wasn't. She didn't say so. Still, I could tell. I knew it wasn't because all of us kids were out of school making noise and messing up the house. She liked it when we were all home.

"Mama, what's wrong with you? Did I do something wrong? Did you like me better when I was another color?"

"Where do you get such outlandish ideas, Beebe?" Mama put her hands on her hips and frowned. "You know I wore out my knees praying for you to get well, and now that you are healthy again, I am blessed. Truly blessed. I wouldn't care if you were polka-dotted so long as you're healthy. There's nothing wrong with me. I'm just a little distracted."

Distracted she might be, but for the last few days, she hadn't been herself. That was for sure. She'd put up a calendar in the kitchen and started to mark off the days with a big "X" each morning when she got up.

"How come you're checking off those days?" I asked her.

"Counting," she told me. "I'm putting them in a treasure box."

"What for? You can't get them back. How can you put them in a treasure box? They're all gone."

"Well, Beebe, you write in your journal. I'll write in the memory book I have in my head. These are special, wonderful, glorious days, and I want to remember everything about them."

Mama picked me up, set me on the kitchen cabinet, and smiled at me. "I love you, Beebe," she said. "You have a good heart. That is an important gift. Not everyone has one. You make sunshine wherever you go." She was smiling, but it wasn't her real smile. This smile was sincere and warm but somehow not quite right. Even a kid can tell when something's not right with her mother's smile. I did like hearing that Mama thought my heart was good. I'd been trying my best not to fall into sin.

In our entryway, the letter still sat on the table unopened. I asked Mama about it every other day or so. She told me I was a nosy little critter and that she would open the letter when she got around to it. She said she wasn't going to open it right that minute or anytime soon and for me to hush up about it.

The summer days moved slowly. Everybody had a routine. Daddy would get up and go to work. Mama would do the wash or sew or prep what she was going to cook for supper. My sister would go play Barbies with her friends or find a shady spot and read a book. Scooter and I spent our days outside, climbing our favorite tree or taking our strings down to the water to catch crabs. Every day that summer was more or less the same. Long, lazy, and endless. Basically, wonderful.

In the evenings, Daddy would come home from work, give Mama a kiss, and either help brush Pat's long brown hair or let me sit on his lap and read the newspaper with him while he smoked his pipe.

"You know, Punkin," he said. "I would be happy to brush your hair too if you had any. I hope you and Sam don't ever play barbershop again. You both look pretty ragged, though I must say I'm glad you were the barber and not your brother. I hate to think of Sam using a pair of scissors, much less clippers."

I ran my hand through the stubby remnants of my hair. If it hadn't rained last week, I might still have long hair. The weather had kept Scooter and me inside, and for something to do we had set up an imaginary barbershop. The results, however, weren't imaginary and left a lot to be desired. Giving ourselves a haircut was one of those things nobody had told us not to do. I would never understand how a kid is supposed to know all this not-to-do stuff? Why hadn't anyone made a list?

Once or twice, I had seen my father look to see if the letter on the entryway table had been opened. It hadn't. The letter had become just part of the assortment of things Mama kept on the little table along with a vase, the Bible, Daddy's pipe, and a box of sweet-smelling tobacco. I had checked the letter several times myself to see if it was still sealed. It was. A few times, I picked around the edges of the flap to see if maybe the South Carolina humidity had loosened the glue. It hadn't, and it didn't. I did write in my journal that my mother's lack of curiosity was driving me crazy. Otherwise, I kept my complaints about the letter to myself.

The days stretched out long and lazy, and the evenings lasted forever and ever that summer. We made homemade ice cream on the porch almost every night, with Scooter sitting on top of the old crank freezer holding down the folded rug on top. His butt—spelled with two *t*s and a word I'm not allowed to say—held the rug in place to keep the ice from melting too fast, while Daddy turned the handle until it wouldn't turn anymore. Mama would bring out a big platter and remove the paddle, and we would take turns licking ice cream off the paddle blades. Someone had to check to see if the ice cream was fit to eat. Daddy and Pat would then pack the freezer with salt and ice and more salt so that the ice cream would set up. You had to wait an eternity for it to get firm—at least an hour—with the sweet taste of the ice cream from the paddles still in your mouth.

In the evenings, when the sun finally went down, the kids on the block would catch fireflies while Mama and Daddy dragged lawn chairs out to visit with the neighbors. Unlike the summer before, the grown-ups always quit talking when any of us kids came around, and they seemed to wait to start up again until we were out of hearing range. That just made me want to hear what they were saying all the more. When people start to whisper, you know it's something you want to hear. When they see you and stop talking, you know you've missed something important—maybe about you, maybe about someone or something else.

I occasionally caught some of what was being said by the grown-ups, but never enough to make any sense out of their conversation. Maybe a word or an occasional tail end of a sentence: ". . . not enough gasoline . . . so young . . . they aren't ready" or "If I only had . . . but you know Congress, they want you to do something with nothing . . . won't give you what you need to do it with . . ."

I overheard Dr. Phil say, "You're the squadron commander. That ought to be worth something."

"Not much," my father replied.

Then I heard my mother say something like, "You do the best you can . . . Korea . . . some experience . . . you've been there."

And then Daddy answered, ". . . trying to train nuggets to . . . without gasoline . . . if only I could give them five more hops, then maybe there's a chance they might be . . . ready."

The whole exchange might as well have been in a foreign language.

CHAPTER 28

M Y DADDY WAS COMMANDING OFFICER of a Marine fighter squadron. I had learned that from one of my friends who lives on our block. "VMA-331," my friend told me, sticking his arms out like wings and running around in a circle making airplane sounds.

"Vroom! Vroom!" he roared.

When Daddy came home from work that evening, I asked him, "What's a *commanding officer?*"

"Well, it's someone who tries to do a lot of everything with a bunch of nothing to make aviators out of rookies who haven't seen the elephant," he said. "Somebody who solves problems with duct tape and chewing gum and teaches pilots to keep their eyes on the meatball when they land on the carrier."

"Are there tigers and zebras, or just elephants?"

"No zebras, but once we had a squadron of Flying Tigers."

"I never saw a tiger fly."

"Neither did I until I joined the Marines, but they'll fly anything if they have enough gasoline."

"Do you have enough gasoline in your squadron?"

"Not enough. Never enough. It costs too much."

"Then how do you fly the planes? I mean, how can you fly them without gasoline?"

"Well, when that happens, we fly on a wing and a prayer. That's what we do. Marines have been flying like that for a long time, so we're good at it; we get a lot of practice. So you have nothing to worry about. When I was in Korea, I never seemed to have enough gas to get back to the landing strip—learned to be ready to make a dead-stick landing when I was coming in from a run. No problem. I did it all the time."

"Where did you get your dead sticks?"

"Well, we had a big tree behind the hanger," he said. "We collected sticks every evening. We had plenty of dead sticks. We made magic wands out of 'em for when we needed to make a dead-stick landing."

I knew he was teasing me. I also knew I wouldn't get a straight answer out of him. So I gave up. I guess if angels could fly without gasoline, then my daddy could too. Nobody in my family ever told me anything important, but I had already figured out on my own that my daddy flew airplanes. He wore wings on his shirt, so I knew.

Mama said she didn't know for absolute sure if Daddy flew airplanes or not—because anybody could pin wings on a shirt. They sold them at the PX. And she refused to find out. She had never once seen Daddy fly, and if she had never actually seen him fly, how could anybody be sure that he did? So as far as she was concerned, Daddy flying airplanes was all hearsay.

I couldn't believe that she had never checked it out, but she hadn't. She seemed satisfied with her logic. As I said earlier, no curiosity. Even when Daddy took Dr. Phil to Philadelphia, Mama had pointed out that all we saw was the two of them in their orange flight suits.

"Anyone can put on a flight suit," Mama said later. "Doesn't prove that you fly, Beebe."

She wouldn't fly herself. She said it wasn't natural.

"Don't you want to go see for yourself?" I asked her.

"Nope," said Mama. "I'm perfectly happy not knowing for sure. He says he does. Who knows? As long as I don't see what he flies, it could be a kite or a balloon."

Sometimes my mother can be difficult to understand, and other times, she borders on irrational. "Mama, Daddy flies planes. He flies them for Uncle Sam! You know he does. Why don't you go see for yourself?" I asked her.

"Now why would I want to do something like that?" Mama said. "Let sleeping dogs lie. That's what I say."

I knew my daddy's nickname was Dawg when he was growing up, but he wasn't asleep right then, and he never told a lie. What did sleeping dogs have to do with flying airplanes? Dogs don't talk, so how could they tell a lie? Mama said the strangest things sometimes. One minute you're talking about flying and the next, you're talking about sleeping dogs that tell lies.

Later that day Andy told me something, and I wished he hadn't.

"It's 'cause pilots sometimes get dead," Andy said. "That's why your mother didn't want to know for sure. They get dead all the time."

"Take that back, Andy! That's not true!" I yelled.

Andy stood his ground: "Is too!"

"Isn't!"

"Is!" Andy hollered. "My dad has to fix them up at the hospital when they jump out of their planes—sometimes they get hurt when their *election* seat fires."

"*Ejection*, not *election*. You're just a little kid! What do you know?"

"I know 'cause my dad says fighter pilots need a psychiatrist because they're certifiably nuts."

"What does certifiably mean?"

"I don't know," Andy said, with a shrug, "but it must be bad."

"You're lying! Fighter pilots don't need anybody, and they don't jump out of airplanes. They fly them and they train animals. I know because my daddy told me his job is to show the rookies the elephants. You're just saying that because your daddy collects brains in jars, and you're jealous. My dad has seen a flying tiger. So there!"

"What's a rookie?"

"Oh, Andy," I said, "you don't know anything about anything. Rooks are blackbirds, and rookies are little birds. Little birds that fly."

Andy looked upset. "Why did you say that about my dad's brain jars, Becky? You like my dad's brain jars. And I'm not jealous, and you know it. Brains are cooler than planes." And with that, Andy turned around and went inside.

I was losing the argument with him anyway, so I didn't go after him. I knew what I knew. I was just upset because Andy sounded like he might know something about pilots getting hurt that I didn't. I needed to check that out. So that night, I asked my father if he really, really, really flew planes? And if he did, was he going to get hurt?

"Well, yes to the first question and of course not to the second. I fly big fast birds. Faster than anything anyone else has. And besides, I'm a fighter pilot in the U.S. Marine Corps—nobody can catch me. And even if they could catch me, they sure couldn't hurt me. I've been in the Marine Corps for more than nineteen years, and nobody has ever caught me, and nobody has ever hurt me. I have an angel on my shoulder and a little girl waiting in the driveway every evening for me. God willing, someday, I'm going to retire and spend my days raising chickens, chewing tobacco, and spitting on the sidewalk."

I gave him a disapproving look. "You don't chew tobacco. It's disgusting. And you aren't supposed to spit—it spreads germs, Mama said so."

"Well, maybe I'll grow a beard, smoke my pipe, and learn how to roller-skate. That's a good thing to know how to do. I've always wanted to learn how to roller-skate."

It felt like he was teasing me, but I couldn't be sure. He looked so serious. "If you grow a beard, you'll get your Cheerios all stuck in it at breakfast. That would be disgusting, Daddy. I think you're teasing me. You already smoke a pipe. Why won't you answer my question? Are the birds you fly dangerous?"

"Only to people who try to hurt me—or you. No one better mess with my Punkin. I'll sic my tiger on them," my father said with a grin.

Our conversation was going nowhere fast, so I asked him about a word he had said that I had never heard before. "What do you mean that you're going to *retire*?" I asked. "What does *retire* mean?"

"*Retire* means you've put in twenty years doing something that is danger . . .," he stopped midword. "What I mean to say is . . . it's like the prize in the Cracker Jack box. You have to stay in long enough and live through . . . no." He hesitated again. "You have to eat all the Cracker Jacks to find the prize at the bottom. Retiring is like the prize at the bottom of the Cracker Jack box. The Marine Corp will give me a little money every month after I retire. Not enough to live on, but enough so that we won't starve until I find another job."

"What other kind of job?"

"I don't exactly know yet," he said. "There aren't any flying jobs out in the real world that I want to do, so I'm thinking about joining the circus—since I already know about tigers and elephants."

I could always tell when I wasn't going to find out anything more from one of my parents, but I was curious enough to try one last question. "How long do you have to be a Marine before you can retire?"

"I'll always be a Marine," he said.

"How long until you retire?"

"Six months after I ask, and I can't ask for another month, not until August nineteenth. That's the day when I will have exactly nineteen and one-half years in—one more month. August the nineteenth, I can put in my letter to retire."

"Are you going to?"

"Going to what?"

"Ask to retire on August the nineteenth."

"Yes, if I don't get orde . . . no, hmm . . . if I don't have to . . . I'll tell you what, Beebe. When I retire, I promise that I won't let Cheerios get stuck in my beard or spit on the sidewalk when anyone is looking."

I must have looked doubtful.

"I'll teach you to spit," he whispered, "if you want to learn how."

"Quit teaching that child such nonsense!" my mother yelled from the kitchen.

My father hadn't given me a good answer. I didn't know much more than I did before. So I just quit worrying about it. He flew airplanes that were big birds. He had a tiger that could fly. He trained rookies at work. They had meatballs on the deck of the carrier to help them land but no spaghetti. Mama could think whatever she wanted to about whether my daddy flew airplanes or not. What did it matter? Daddy was retiring in a month to raise chickens, teach me to spit, and learn how to roller-skate. I was a good roller skater; maybe I could teach him. I wasn't too sure, however, about the chewing tobacco. I didn't think Mama would like Daddy chewing tobacco and spitting on the sidewalk.

I know for sure what she would say about me learning to spit.

CHAPTER 29

THE SUMMER DRIFTED by, lazy and wonderful—except for the letter still sitting unopened on the table. "Mama, please open the letter," I said, carrying it into the kitchen where she was making a cake for dinner. "Please! I can't stand it anymore. I think I'm going to die of curiosity! Why do you let it lie there day after day? Don't you want to know what's in it?"

"Hmmm, okay, maybe I will open it, maybe, this evening after supper. We'll see. Could you please take a look at the calendar and tell me what day it is? August the what? While you're doing that, stick your finger in the cake batter and see if it tastes like it should. If it's any good, get us a couple of spoons."

"What difference does it make what day it is?" I asked as I stuck my finger in the batter, licked it clean, and went in search of two spoons.

Mama set the bowl down on the kitchen table, and we took turns dipping our spoons in the batter. Mama's cakes were always smaller than normal cakes because she made sure the batter was fit to eat before we baked the cake. Some mothers might bake bigger cakes, but they probably were going to poison their families someday because they weren't careful about checking the batter.

Between spoonfuls, I asked again, "Mama, why do you care what the date is?"

She sighed. "Because I don't want to open that letter one single day sooner than I have to. I really truly don't."

I latched onto the part of her answer that mattered: She might open the letter! I might soon know what was inside!

By now, the letter had been lying on our entry table since the first week in June, and now it was the first week in August. Still, something about the way Mama said she might open the letter just now made it sound as if she already knew what was in it. How could that be? This was the first time I had made any headway on the letter opening. I pressed my advantage.

"Mama, do you already know what the letter says? Is that why you haven't opened it?"

"No, I don't know for sure what it says, but I know what it means. When I open it, our lives could . . . might . . . change, and I don't want that to happen right now. I don't like to worry about things before I absolutely have to. And anyway, maybe it won't be what I think it is and I won't have to worry at all. Now that I think about it, maybe I'm not ready to find out what's in the letter today. And as long as we are discussing it, *no*."

"No, what?" I asked.

"No! I'm not going to talk about what's in it or what might be in it, and if you don't hush about that letter and put it back where you got it, I'll wait another week. Or maybe I won't open it at all. I don't ever have to open it if I don't want to. As a matter of fact, I don't think I want to. I've changed my mind. I'm not opening it. I'm busy baking this cake."

With that, Mama picked up the bowl of cake batter and poured what remained into a greased pan already dusted with flour, and that was the end of that. There would be no more talk about the letter. I knew my mama. Done. Finished. Over. I knew when I was beaten. I had been there plenty of times before. Sometimes I say just one word too many. Sometimes I say a bucketful too many. When you're a little kid, you haven't had enough practice to know exactly when you should shut up and stop talking. Obviously I needed more practice on such things, but I was beginning to catch on. I had learned the only way to figure out where the line is, was to keep talking until you crossed it, so the next time you could try to remember where the line was. The problem for me was that Mama and Daddy have different lines on different days—sometimes on the same day, which complicated everything. Staying on the right side of the line was an art, and way too much to expect from a little kid like me.

By nature, though, I'm an optimist, and Mama hadn't said for sure she wouldn't open the letter later that evening. So maybe after supper? I would have to wait it out. You know how time can stretch until every minute seems as if it lasts a year or more? You look up at the clock after moping around for what seems like an hour, and find that the big hand on the clock has moved only a minute. The whole rest of my day was like that. When you are waiting to see whether something is going to happen or not, time stands still. The hands on the clock don't move.

Instead of putting the envelope back on the entry table, I slid it between the salt and pepper shakers on the old oak table when I set it that evening for dinner, right where Mama couldn't help but see it. I wasn't going to say another word about it. I might not know where the line was, but I knew for sure when I had crossed it. After the table was set, I went out to sit by the driveway and wait for Daddy to come home.

I passed Pat on the front porch playing Barbie dolls with her friends. My sister liked horses, cats, and every other kind of animal in the world—dogs, gerbils, white mice, and turtles, but hurt animals were her favorites. She continually dragged home creatures that were wounded or near death's door, wrapped them in bandages, and then either healed or killed them with tender affection. We always had some hurt animal that needed her attention lying on a towel in a box in the kitchen. Pat is my sister, but we came from different planets. She played with dolls. I climbed trees. She nursed wounded animals. I caught crabs—to eat, with nary a thought of nursing them back to health. That about sums it up. Guess it takes all kinds of people to make up a family.

Thank goodness for my little brother. Scooter took after me. Loud, but okay. Pat was okay too, but never got into trouble. She liked to do calm, quiet things. That's okay if you like that sorta stuff. I don't.

I tried to play with dolls once. It did not take. Scooter and I, on the other hand, stayed in trouble. I couldn't always say which one of us got us there, but before most days were over, we usually both seemed to find our way into trouble, one way or the other. Mama told us things we shouldn't do, which we didn't do. It was the things she didn't cover that caused most of the problems. Once Mama told us not to put our fingers in light sockets. So we didn't. But there are a million other things you can stick in a light socket besides your fingers. Sterling-silver butter knives, for instance. I stuck one of Mama's in a socket in the kitchen to see what would happen. Thanks to Daddy and the electrical sparks, I learned about fusion and conductivity and the melting point of silver. We now butter our bread with a sterling-silver butter knife that has a blackened, melted notch between the handle and the blade.

"Let me clarify something for you, Beebe," Mama had said. "Don't put anything in a light socket—ever. Do you understand?"

I nodded. I got it. New rule.

On the way to my waiting spot by our driveway, as I passed by Pat, I paused to ask her, "Did Mama tell you why she won't open the letter?"

"What letter?" Pat asked as she pulled a pink hand-knitted dress over Barbie's head and reached in her little Barbie suitcase for the matching pink shoes. Neither my sister nor her friend even looked up. Pat and her friends had completed third grade. I had not. Enough said.

"You know what letter!" I shouted. "The one that has been lying on the table for the last two months—unopened!"

"No, I don't know. And you don't have to yell, Idgit. I saw the letter, but it wasn't for me—or for you either. So what's the problem? It's Mama's letter not yours."

I stomped the rest of the way to my waiting-for-Daddy spot and plopped down on the ground. My whole family was impossible. Sometimes I thought I must have come from the Piggly Wiggly instead of the PX like my brother. Or maybe I was an alien. Or maybe they had mixed me up with some other kid and I was in the wrong family. Everyone in my family sat around and thought and discussed things. I was the only one who ever tried things out without all the thinking and discussing. I couldn't remember the last time anyone in my family had done anything interesting without thinking first. Except for Scooter. I was teaching him everything I knew as fast as I could, so I still had hope for him.

Settled on the grass in my usual spot, I found a twig on the lawn and began poking the closest anthill. I watched as the ants poured out, carrying their eggs with them, trying to go who knows where. The sun was already going down when I realized my father was late—very late. I ran into the house and yelled to Mama, "Daddy's late!"

"I know, I know. He called. He's going down south for a little vacation and won't be home tonight."

"Where south?"

"South-south."

"How come he gets to go everywhere interesting and we don't? How come the Marine Corps never invites us to go anywhere with him?" I don't know why I bothered to ask. I already knew the answer. I had heard Daddy say it enough times: *If the Marines wanted me to have a wife and children, they would have issued them to me when I joined.*

"I'm sorry, Beebe. I should have called you in and told you," Mama said. "I forgot you were sitting out there waiting on him. Come on— let me get your supper for you." She had already folded the leaves back down on the table, put the china back in the cabinet, and set the dinette table in the kitchen for us. The letter was nowhere to be seen.

"Hop up to the table, and I'll fix you a plate," Mama said.

I was still dying to know where the letter had gone, but I'm not stupid. "Why can't we go on vacation with Daddy? I can't remember the last time he took us on vacation with him."

"Because we can't. It's a Marine vacation. They're taking their airplanes to play with, and we would only be in the way."

"See! I told you he flew airplanes! You just said he had an airplane. I heard it. You said it. You said that he flies airplanes."

She didn't take the bait, so I tried a different tactic. "When's he coming home?"

"Shhh. We'll know when he gets here."

"Where's he at?"

"Don't end a sentence with a preposition."

"Okay, where is he? *At*."

"Roosevelt Roads."

"Is that in South Carolina?"

"Beebe, shhh. No more questions, please."

"One more—just one more, Mama?"

"Okay, one more. I'm too tired to argue with you about it."

"Is Daddy retiring? He said he can ask to retire when he has nineteen-and-a-half years in the Marine Corps. And the other day, he said that he has been in for almost nineteen-and-a-half years. Is he retiring?"

"Well, yes and no. You can't put in a request to retire until you've served a full nineteen-and-a-half years. He will finish his nineteen-and-a-half years on the nineteenth of August, and then he can ask to retire. That doesn't happen for another two weeks. Then, God willing, he'll retire. Unless, of course, he gets orders first."

"Will he?"

"Will he what?"

"Get orders first."

"No! Surely, they wouldn't give him orders with only six months to go. I'm sure the Marine Corps wouldn't . . . Beebe . . . well, surely . . ."

Mama took a deep breath.

"Surely they wouldn't do that."

CHAPTER 30

M Y DADDY CAME HOME from Roosevelt Roads, and life returned to normal. When Daddy wasn't home, we ate off the stove in the kitchen. When he was home, we used sterling silver tableware and linen napkins, ate in the dining room, and Mama served everything in pink china bowls. All of our dishes were pink. Mama said that was because in the fifties when she and Daddy got married, everything anyone bought was pink—pink hats, pink hair dryers . . . pink, pink, pink . . . pink poodles on felt skirts. Mama still had her pink poodle skirt, of course, because she never threw anything away. Pat and I spent many an afternoon playing dress up in it.

The sterling silver set was a present from my father. He had given it to Mama to celebrate him getting renamed. Yes, the Marines had given Daddy a new first name again. His real name, E. Kenneth Jacks, never changed, Mama said, but his new Marine name was Lieutenant Colonel instead of Major.

"How come they changed your name to Lieutenant Colonel?" I asked my father.

"Becky, you are a doodle-dandy. Lieutenant Colonel, huh? Well, that's not actually my first name, my real first name is E."

"Then why do all the men call you 'Lieutenant Colonel' if that isn't your first name? And what kind of name is *E* anyway? What does the *E* stand for, Daddy?"

"Can't tell you. It's a secret. My friends call me Ken. Hop up here on the step, and let's forget about names and read the newspaper. Just look at all the men in the obituaries with first names. And see, they all kicked the bucket. Nobody kicked the bucket who had a single letter for their first name, so you can see why I don't want a first name; all I need is a letter. First names get a fella in trouble. And would you believe it, it says right here in the Beaufort newspaper that all the women with first names have to go to baby showers."

"You're teasing me."

"I wouldn't do that!" he said.

"Yes, you would."

"Wouldn't!"

"Would!" After exchanging a few woulds and wouldn'ts, I tend to forget what I'm arguing about; Daddy had turned to my favorite comic strip, so I sat down beside him and we read it together. I didn't care about his first name. I was always gonna call him Daddy anyway.

The next week, Daddy went on vacation to Roosevelt Roads again, and we ate on paper plates that night. Daddy was gone but so was something else.

"Where's my pink plate?" I asked, looking around. "Hey, all the pink plates are missing from the china cabinet! So are the pink bowls! The cabinet is empty!"

"Packed," my mother said without even looking up.

"Why? Why did you pack the pink plates and bowls?"

Silence.

"Come on, Mama. Please, tell me. Why did you pack the pink plates? Where did you put them?"

Silence.

I knew I might as well stop asking. There would be no answers for me. Sometimes I hate being a kid.

That night after supper I looked for the letter.

It was gone too. Nowhere to be found.

CHAPTER 31

"DO YOU REMEMBER THAT bad thing you said about pilots?" I asked Andy. "Well, you're wrong! I told my daddy what you said, and he told me he won't get hurt 'cause he doesn't have a first name." I took a deep breath. "You have to have a first name to get in an obituary. He only has a first letter, so he will be fine."

"He does too have a first name," Andy said.

"He does not."

"Does too."

"Does not!" I hollered.

"Does too!" Andy said. "Everybody has a first name. It's a rule."

I stalked off. Andy had had the last word again, but what did he know? I could read. Andy couldn't. And I knew what I knew. I had read the Beaufort newspaper for myself. The only way you could get in an obituary was if you had a first name.

When I got back to our house, I found my mother reading a book, a highly unusual sight during the day but especially in the middle of the afternoon. She usually started supper about this time. I stomped over to her, still irritated with Andy.

"What's for supper, Mama?"

Silence.

She didn't even bother to look up from the page.

"Is Daddy coming home from his vacation tonight in time to eat? I can set the table. You want to tell me where you put the pink plates so I can set the table?"

"No, I don't. Not tonight."

"Why?"

"Your father and some of his friends went to Roosevelt Roads again and are still there. They're going to stay and play on the beach for a while. The President is paying for all of them to have a vacation, so it might be a few days. He'll be home when he gets home. In the meantime, tell me what your favorite thing is to eat, and we'll fix it."

Not a word about where the pink plates had gone! Had Mama grown tired of pink?

"I want fried chicken," I told her. "Smashed potatoes and gravy—and yellow pie."

"Coconut or lemon?"

"The kind that's sour."

"That's lemon. Give me an hour to finish this chapter, and I'll cut up the chicken, and you can squeeze the lemons for the pie."

"Can we have fried okra too?"

"You know, they might grow okra here, but I haven't found any to buy since we left Oklahoma. Now go on, Beebe—and hush. I'm trying to concentrate on this book. Go play somewhere else for a little while."

This person was not my mother. But I gave her an hour before I tried bugging her again about the pink plates. She just ignored me again and went on reading as if I wasn't even there. I gave up. Sooner than usual. Guess Andy had left me argued out.

Finally, Mama closed her book and went into the kitchen to start supper. Mama's chicken always has a pulley bone, what some people call a *wishbone*. You have to cut up the chicken in a certain way to get a pulley bone. You can't get one at most restaurants because the cooks hack their chickens into pieces with a wood ax before they fry them. Daddy told me that, the part about the hacking them with an ax. Mama told him to quit telling me such nonsense. She says that to him a lot. I don't know what she was so worried about. We don't own an ax.

After Mama fried the chicken in her cast-iron skillet, we sat down to eat. Before anyone could take a bite, Scooter started rubbing gravy in his hair. Some gravy did make it into his mouth, but he smeared most of it on his head, which made his hair stand on end in spikes. If he was hoping that Pat and I would reward him with a giggle, he succeeded, which only encouraged him to rub more gravy in his hair.

Scooter has a talent for making people laugh, but on this night, Mama was not laughing. In fact, Mama didn't even seem to notice his antics, which was again unusual. Instead, without a word, she picked Scooter up, hauled him to the bathroom, and plopped him into the bathtub as if a gravy hairdo happened every day.

Don't sweat the small stuff had always been one of my mother's favorite sayings. As for me, I find it hard to keep up with what's small and what isn't around here.

CHAPTER 32

THE NEXT MORNING, A MAN in uniform showed up at our front door and rang the doorbell. When no one answered, he began to knock. I peered through the peephole to see who it was, but it was somebody I didn't know, and I wasn't allowed to open the door for strangers. Don't open the door to strangers was near the top of Mama's list of things not to do.

The stranger wore a cross on his uniform. I had seen this kind of man before but never at our house. We went to a church outside the gate. We didn't have a *military churchman*; we had a *preacher man*.

"Mama!" I yelled. "There's a churchman banging on our door."

I heard a crash from the kitchen where Mama was snapping beans. Not a sound after that and no Mama.

The knocking at the door started again.

"Mama?" I hollered. "Did you hear me?"

Mama emerged from the kitchen and walked straight to the front door, only to stop. She stared at the door for what felt like a long time, then stepped closer and looked through the glass. The man on the other side looked right back at her. I had never seen my mother act like this before. "Aren't you going to open the door?" I whispered to her.

Mama turned to look at me as if she hadn't realized I was there. The man knocked again.

"Are you going to let him in?" I asked.

"No, no, I'm not. He's not coming in here." Then she yelled at the man through the closed door. "Go away! I don't want to talk to you. Just go away!"

She had gone so pale I thought she might faint.

"What's wrong with you, Mama?" I had never heard Mama be rude to someone like that before. She was never rude—even to rude strangers. "Aren't you going to let him in?"

"No, I am not," she said. "He can stand out there all day. I'm not letting him in this house and I'm not talking to him!"

With that, she turned and returned to the kitchen. The man with the cross on his uniform remained on the porch for a while longer, then finally gave up and retreated.

Mama wasn't herself for the rest of the day. We ate peanut-butter sandwiches for supper. Pat mixed peanut butter with real butter and molasses in a bowl and slathered the mixture on slices of bread. She used molasses because we didn't have any jelly. Running out of jelly was strange. We always had a jar of jelly in the cupboard. Stranger still, the pantry had hardly any jars or cans of anything else. The pantry was almost empty. So was the refrigerator.

Scooter tried his peanut-butter-in-the-hair routine again during dinner, but this time nobody even smiled. Not even me. Mama just got up from the table and said: "Pat, would you put your brother in the bathtub, please, and don't let him out until he doesn't stick to anything? Becky, would you mind cleaning up the dishes?" Then she turned around and said, "Scott Jacks, if you ever rub food in your hair again, I'll spank you!"

Scooter's jaw dropped, but Mama didn't even look back. She went straight to her bedroom, shut the door, and didn't come back out for what felt like hours. That was the first time I had ever heard Mama call my brother by his real name. It was pretty scary. A little before bedtime she finally reappeared but only to ask, "Beebe, did the phone ring while I was lying down? Did the churchman come back?"

There were dark circles under Mama's eyes, and her eyes were red as if she had been crying. Of course that wasn't possible; our mother never, never cried. "You can cry if you want," she once told Pat and me, "but it doesn't accomplish a thing except to upset everyone else. When something goes wrong, it's better to take your licks, pick yourself up, and get on with whatever you're doing." Daddy says Mama is a tough old tenderhearted cookie. Whatever that means. I have a hard time understanding half of what either one of them is saying to the other sometimes.

"No, Mama," I said, "the phone didn't ring, and no one came to the front door either."

If I had thought she might explain what prompted her question, I was wrong. Without another word, she headed to the kitchen and started making corn bread. She put a pot of beans on the back burner of the stove as if nothing had happened, and when the Beaufort newspaper came that evening, Mama was the first one out the door to get it. She came back inside, sank into a corner of the sofa, and read the paper from cover to cover. When she finished, she smiled, threw the paper into the garbage, turned the beans on to simmer, and took us all out for ice cream—banana splits with hot fudge, whipped cream, and nuts with a cherry on top. Jeanette and Andy went with us too, and for once, Andy didn't blab nonsense the whole time.

Later that evening, I heard Mama on the phone to the churchman, "I'm sorry I wouldn't let you in this morning, but I thought . . . it wasn't until I read the newspaper—"

He must have interrupted her, because she stopped mid-sentence. And that's when I did a real bad sin. I picked up the extension phone and put it to my ear, something definitely absolutely on Mama's list of things not to do.

"I'm new. I was just checking in to introduce myself," he said. "I wanted to meet all the officers and wives in your husband's squadron. Back in the Midwest where I come from, a pastor calls on his people. I didn't even think. You were the first call I made. I thought I'd start with the commanding officer's family. I'll know to call next time before I go to someone's house and let them know my visit is only a courtesy call—just to say hello. I'm very sorry and do hope you will forgive me. I didn't realize what a chaplain's uniform showing up at the door would mean to you. I didn't think about the squadron being deployed. I will now, and I hope you will let me visit sometime when it would not be a bother. I hope you'll let me try again."

"Of course you can stop by," Mama said. "Give me a call and a definite time, so I don't have to wonder why you're at my front door. I'm sorry for acting the way I did, and I'm glad you understand."

"Three o'clock tomorrow is a good time for me," the chaplain said. "Would that be a good time for you?"

"I'll have cookies waiting for you." Mama hung up the phone, ran her fingers through her hair, and started to hum a song we sometimes sang at church. My mother was happy again.

I hung up the extension phone and slipped out the back door before she could figure out that I had listened in on her conversation. I headed to the hideout that Scooter and I had made underneath the big azalea bush behind the porch. The ground there was covered with Spanish moss as soft as a carpet. Only an occasional splatter of light broke through the leaves. We liked to go there and pretend we were bears hibernating for the winter. It was usually a great place to think too. But on this evening, I was restless—feeling guilty for eavesdropping on my mother because eavesdropping was most certainly on her don't-do list.

Unfortunately, curiosity is my weakness, and it had led me into trouble again.

CHAPTER 33

I WAS FEELING GUILTY ABOUT eavesdropping on Mama's phone call and decided I had better not wait until bedtime to say my prayers. I sent a quick one up to God.

> *Now God, you need to listen to me. I would appreciate it if you would quit putting all these temptations in my way. It's going to get me into real trouble someday. You're supposed to not lead me into temptation, but you just keep doing it! I truly don't want to sin and change colors again. I listened in on the phone because that churchman had made Mama so upset—I had to know what they were saying. I need to know such things. I'm sure you understand. Amen.*

I probably didn't have my religion exactly right about who was to blame when I did something I shouldn't have done. Still feeling a little guilty, I went inside and called out, "Mama, where are you?"

"Here in the utility room folding clothes. Do you have something you want to tell me, Beebe?"

Now, how did she know that? Do mothers have a special radar where their children are concerned? Realizing there was no easy way to confess what I had done and get it off the heavenly books, I just came clean: "Well, Mama, I accidentally sort of picked up the phone when you were talking to the churchman, and well, I kinda listened, but just for a little bit."

"*Accidentally*, you say. And just for a little bit—like until I hung up the phone?" Mama said.

"Uh-huh. I needed to know what that man was telling you."

"You know eavesdropping is rude, Beebe."

"Uh-huh."

"What do you think a mother should do with a child who not only disobeys but is also rude?"

"Well, I think if she is a good mother . . . she will know how sorry I am . . . and will bake those cookies for the chaplain and not let me eat any of the dough."

"Well, that'd certainly be an original form of punishment," she said.

"You and Pat and Scooter could eat the cookie dough all by yourselves," I said, "and not share any of it with me."

"Now what fun would that be, eating cookie dough without you?"

"Well, maybe I could help you all eat the dough so you wouldn't be too lonely, and that would be a good deed to cancel out my bad one?"

"I don't believe that makes much sense," she said. "Seems to me you have just circled your transgression, eaten the cookie dough, and tossed the punishment to boot. Don't you think?"

"Well, Mama, I don't know what you should do with a kid like me that's curious about everything. I already told God that he should stop leading me into temptation if he expects me to be good."

"Oh, you did, did you." Mama clamped a hand over her mouth and turned her face away from me, something she had told us never—ever—to do. It was on the don't-do list! You're always supposed to look people in the eye when you speak to them.

"Excuse me," Mama said when she finally turned back to face me. "Where did you come up with the idea that God was the one leading you into temptation? And could you please explain to me how your picking up the phone on purpose and then listening to *my* phone call was God's fault?"

"I learned it from The Lord's Prayer—'Give us this day our daily bread and *lead us not into temptation.*' It's pretty clear. The prayer says he shouldn't lead us into temptation. 'Lead us *not* into temptation,' that's what it says. So it sounds to me like God has a choice as to whether to lead you into it or not. So if I'm tempted to do something my mother told me not to do . . . I think then God's partly to blame 'cause I'm just a little kid. And I don't know how to resist temptation very well. And besides, it is hard for little kids to resist temptation. We need practice on how to resist stuff before we can do it. He should know that."

Mama was staring at me like I was a goofball by now. I watched as she inhaled slowly, and then looked me straight in the eye.

She was not smiling.

"Well, now, Beebe, that is some mighty fancy interpretation of scripture. You have part of it right. It is hard to resist temptation—for everyone. However, for all your stretching and twisting of the Bible's words to fit the deed, I'm afraid you have it backward. It isn't God that tempts you. The Bible says, 'God tempts no man.' . . . "

I interrupted—even though I knew interrupting was also high up on the don't-do list: "The Bible doesn't say anything about little kids, though, does it, Mama? Maybe he tempts little kids to help them learn how to resist temptation."

"No! Absolutely not! The devil tempts you, not God. But the devil doesn't make you do it. You do it all by yourself. You were tempted to do something you weren't supposed to do. And you did it. *You*—not God, not the devil—you!"

"Well, I think the Bible should be a little bit clearer about what it says, and then I wouldn't get messed up about what it means." I checked her expression. I could tell things weren't going well for me.

"Rebecca—you did it!"

Using my full name was not a good sign. Neither was the way she slowly articulated every syllable. "This was not—not!—God's fault. This was not—not!—the Bible's fault. This was your fault! I told you listening in on another person's conversations on the phone is rude, and you still reached your little hand out and lifted the receiver and put it to your sweet little ear and listened. You—you!—are the one who eavesdropped. Get me?"

I might not have understood what The Lord's Prayer said on the subject, but I was very clear where Mama stood on the matter. Once again, I could see that this conversation was going to go on forever unless I admitted I had done something wrong. Maybe this could still end up with cookie batter for everyone.

"Yes! Yes! I get it, Mama!" Once I said it, I felt relieved to have it behind me. "Next time I'll try harder to keep my fingers from doing wrong."

"No, Beebe, that's not good enough. It wasn't your fingers."

I was still thinking about the cookie batter, and I knew that look on my mother's face. "I did it! I made a bad choice," I said.

"Nope, I'm not buying it," Mama said.

Her tone told me I would not be wiggling out of this one. So to keep the torture of this conversation from going on forever, I took a deep breath and gave in.

"Okay, okay, Mama—I did a bad choice. I disobeyed. It's my fault and I'm sorry. I promise I won't ever do it again!" I blurted the apology out all in one breath so that it wasn't quite so painful.

Mama replied, "God calls it a *sin* when you disobey, not a bad choice. However, thank you. I forgive you. Now you might want to go back to your room and find out how God feels about being accused of doing something he didn't do—but *you* did. Sometimes it helps if you get on your knees and get humble when you talk to him. Especially when you're the one who has done the something wrong. 'Fess up when you're guilty; that's my suggestion. I'm pretty sure that God is waiting to hear from you."

Defeated, I turned to go. At times like these, I wished she would just spank me and send me to my room. I hate having to admit I am wrong. I hate it even more when I know Mama is disappointed in me.

God is more understanding than Mama.

CHAPTER 34

Pryor, Oklahoma
August 2010

I HAD RETURNED TO CLEANING my childhood bedroom, pushing myself to finish and trying to ignore distractions. Three full trash bags were by the bed ready to be carried out when my mother stuck her head in the door.

"You certainly look pensive, Becky—deep in thought about something?" Mama stood in the doorway wiping her hands on a tea towel. Her face was powdered with a dusting of flour, as was the front of her apron. "Are you hungry by any chance?"

"Starving!" I replied. "I got a little sidetracked. I was sitting in here remembering how you used to send me to my room when I did something I wasn't supposed to do."

Mama smiled.

"What are you grinning about?" I asked.

"I didn't know I was," she said, her smile growing wider.

"You were—you are!"

"That's because it's funny."

"Okay, okay," I said. Now I was grinning too. "I was thinking about the time I listened in on your phone call with the chaplain when we lived in South Carolina. You sent me to my room to talk to God about what I'd done. Talking to God was easy back then. 'Now, God,' that's how I always started my prayers. 'You listen to me very carefully,' I would tell him. 'I'm trying to be good, but you make it all too hard for me.' I imagine he liked talking to me back then better than he does now. I was much less muddled in my thinking. Adults make everything too complicated."

Mama chuckled. "Your explanation about temptation that day was so convoluted that I could hardly keep a straight face while you explained it to me. You got so serious at one point that I had to turn around so you wouldn't see me smiling. I'm sure God himself was finding it difficult not to smile."

"Glad I was entertaining at least," I said.

"You certainly were that," Mama said, smiling. "I'm sure God enjoys children better than adults. It is harder when you're grown."

"Yes. Yes, it is."

I picked up the bags of trash, handed her one to carry, and headed to the garage, leaving my journal on the bed.

CHAPTER 35

THE DAY AFTER MAMA TOLD the chaplain to go away, he rang our doorbell at three o'clock sharp. Mama let him in and fed him cookies as if nothing had happened. After he left, we all went to the beach. Andy and Jeanette came too. The tide was going out, so the sand was clean and seashells had washed up along the shoreline. We doused ourselves in sunscreen from head to toe, and then ran into the water, jumping over the waves and yelling at the top of our voices. Mama and Jeanette spread old quilts on the beach to make a soft table for us, the picnic baskets brimming with sandwiches and thermos jugs of sweet tea.

Sometimes God lets you have a perfect day. That day was such a day. We built sandcastles, picked up seashells, and after we grew tired of castles and shells, buried one another in the sand. We ate too much, got too much sun, and played in the ocean until the waves beat us to a pulp. Later, as the sun was going down, Mama and Jeanette packed everything up, and all of us kids climbed into the car. We fell asleep on the way home, tired beyond exhaustion.

Have you ever, in the first few seconds of sleep—right before you leave the world of awake—heard someone talking? I did that day. I was too tired to tell if I was awake or dreaming, but I definitely heard some-one say, ". . . soon . . . maybe a couple of more weeks . . . no, I haven't told them . . . too much sadness for little children. . . . Why should . . ."

I don't remember anything else I heard or didn't hear.

Or that was said.

Or that I dreamed.

My father finally came back from his vacation at the beach with his friends. He brought us seashells, ones different from any we had ever seen on the beach.

"What did you do on vacation?" I asked him.

"We played with our airplanes and ate seafood and picked up shells on the beach."

"Can I go with you next time?" I asked. "I like vacations!"

"Sure. I'll drop a letter in the mail to the President and see if that's okay with him. And if it is, then next time, I'll take you with me. You can help me address the envelope to the White House. But in case he doesn't say yes, what's your second choice?"

That didn't take much thought. "I'd like to go to Oklahoma and see Nana and Poppy and catch tadpoles in Saline Creek. And frogs. I'd like to catch some frogs."

"I think that's doable!" Daddy said.

"Did you go to Saline Creek when you were a little kid like me?"

"No, can't say I ever did," he said. "When I was little, we lived out in western Oklahoma where it's flat and dry. We didn't have a Saline Creek full of frogs."

"That's too bad," I said. "The creek is so much fun."

Saline Creek is full of little bitty snails—millions and zillions of them. Moss grows on the rocks along the water by the banks, and watercress grows in pools where the water is still. All of the water comes from a spring and is freezing cold and so clear you can stand in it up to your chin and count your toes. Not like the water here. The bottom is all pebbles. No sand. It is my most favorite place in the world.

As happy as I was about our Oklahoma plan, something about it was bothering me. I had to ask.

"Daddy, every time we go there, you've been away someplace else. I don't just want to go on vacation to Oklahoma, I want you to go with us this time and catch tadpoles with me in Saline Creek."

"Okay!" my father said. "You've got it! We'll do it the last week in August, and that is a promise. We'll make it our secret. Mama and Pat and Scooter will be surprised when we tell them where we're going and what we're gonna do. And I will very much look forward to helping you catch a critter of some sort in Saline Creek."

To say that I was excited about this doesn't begin to describe it. I can't keep secrets, but I kept this one. It was hard too. Humongously hard. I always want to tell everyone what I'm thinking while I'm thinking it! But because Daddy said to keep this a secret, I bit my tongue and kept my mouth shut. I didn't tell anyone that we were going on vacation in Oklahoma at the end of August . . . with Daddy!

CHAPTER 36

THAT SUMMER, WE WERE NO longer dirt-poor anymore, but we had no *real money*, as Mama put it. Then again, people in Beaufort didn't seem to have much of the real kind either. Folks in Beaufort lived in hand-me-down mansions that they couldn't afford. Taxes were a problem. Paying people to help keep things up was a problem. Keeping furniture waxed and silver shined was a problem as well, so people invented ways to keep things going. In the winter, they rented rooms in their mansions to blue-haired ladies from up north, Yankees escaping the bitter cold winters or folks wanting to experience summer by the seashore. Beautiful, scrumptious meals were served on cutwork linens with fine china, crystal, and sterling.

Servants performed many of the tasks as they had always done. They carried silver trays loaded with food to the table for the white folks and cleaned up the mess after dinner. Northern white folks, southern white folks—no difference. White was still white, and black was still black in the 1960s in much of the South.

On occasion, dinner in one of the homes would become available for a few extra guests. If residents left to visit family or take a trip, their chairs at the table would open up. You had to sign up days in advance and then wait until an hour or two before dinnertime to see if the extra seats would actually be free that evening. It gave a whole new meaning to *last-minute reservation*. That summer Mama called every day for weeks before we finally got one.

"Act civilized or you are never coming with us again," Mama said. "Use a fork. Put your napkin in your lap. Speak nicely to the ladies who spend the winters here. Oh, good grief—you children just try to be polite for an hour. Try not to embarrass us."

The old southern mansion was magical. Crystal chandeliers hung in every room, and candles burned in silver candlesticks on the massive carved sideboards. Cut glass cast sparkles on every surface, and the beveled mirrors held dancing rainbows from a vanishing past. We had a wonderful time that night eating prime rib and being waited on as if we were somebody. We might have been traveling trash to Southern society, but that night, we were served like royalty.

"Money is money," Daddy said, "and they need ours."

Our dinner companions for the evening were several Northerners who had come south to escape the cold and stay in an antebellum mansion. They enjoyed meals served Southern style, each course on a silver platter, carried by servants whose families had worked for nothing only a few years before. Now those servers were paid a wage—a paltry one, according to Mama. Unfortunately, most of them had nowhere else to go for work. These withering antebellum leftovers from the way life had been before the Civil War continued to exist, because served and servers alike were stuck with each other.

Some of the old-timers in Beaufort had parents who had died in what the Confederate government preferred to call the War Between the States, because that sounded like a war between equals and not against one's country. If you wanted to be part of Beaufort society, it helped to have a relative who had served in the military—for the South, of course. If you had a relative who had fought for the North, best to keep that to yourself; at this time in the South, it was still better to be a communist than a Yankee. Yet there was no denying that summer that things were beginning to change. Everywhere you looked, Southern treasure was being discarded. Silver trays, silver bowls—there was no one to shine them anymore. Ballerina girls with airy blown-glass skirts covered with years and years of dust—no one to dust them. Double-tiered compotes, shelves of cut glass, and furniture that needed to be waxed or polished all sat in front yards—no one to wax or polish them. Walnut, cherry, with silver and Dresden, stacked on the long and round tables with signs that read, "For Sale" or "Make an Offer."

For Mama, who had always had an eye for beauty, these sales were irresistible. "Beautiful things will always be in style," she liked to say, "and we women have an obsession with beauty. I'm afraid that we are totally, completely obsessed with it."

At least, we three were—Mama, Pat, and me.

Once again, during those last weeks in Beaufort, just as we had done in Virginia, we took to rising early in the mornings to go looking. Armed with flashlights, we set out to see what dusty treasure we could find for sale in the rundown, overgrown yards of the dying South.

CHAPTER 37

WITH JULY ALMOST OVER, I had begun to worry about school. I was hoping second grade would be more interesting than first had been. One evening while reading the newspaper on the Golfeders' front porch, Dr. Phil had told me that school wasn't made for smart kids. He said smart kids usually had to learn whatever they wanted to know all by themselves. And if they couldn't figure out how to do that, their lives—no matter how smart they were—would be very boring. He didn't actually say I was one of the smart kids, but he did say, "You have a way of soaking up information, Rebecca. So soak up as much as you can on your own."

I had told Dr. Phil about the day the teacher didn't believe me about my sister being in Arlington, how she made me stay after class and write something that wasn't true on the blackboard. "Well, give her what she wants without giving up your soul," Dr. Phil said, "or telling a lie."

"You gave up your soul," I reminded him. "You sold it to the Navy."

"Yes, but that was for a good cause," Dr. Phil said. "The Navy paid for me to go to medical school. However, I'd suggest that if you ever have to give up your soul, make sure you give it to God and not the Navy. God will take better care of it than the Navy ever would."

Then he leaned down and said, "Rebecca, one way to keep from giving up your soul is to keep your mouth shut when your teacher asks a question that you know the answer to—and you know it isn't one she's going to agree with. Instead, look at her, hesitate, and smile. She'll think you don't know the answer and ask somebody else."

"You don't keep your mouth shut very much," I said.

I wasn't being rude, just observant. Everyone knew Dr. Phil liked to talk, but I don't think he even heard me. He seemed to still be thinking about where he had lost his soul. "Medical school—now that was a true learning experience," he said. "You learn to say as little as possible and to live without any sleep."

"You had to sleep sometime," I said.

"Yes, but on my feet with my eyes open."

Since Dr. Phil always talked to me like I was halfway smart, I didn't like to disappoint him. The truth is, I think I soak up so much information because I'm nosy. I filed Dr. Phil's advice away and told myself that surely second grade couldn't possibly be any more boring than first grade had been. There would probably be some new kids, and I had made some friends in first grade who hadn't moved away yet. Maybe some of them would still be there when school started. Orders are a part of life for military kids; every family gets them but not every year. Maybe no one else would get orders this summer. There was always a chance that some of my friends would be back.

When I got home from Dr. Phil's house, Mama was standing in the kitchen with an envelope in one hand and a piece of paper in the other.

"You opened it!" I exclaimed.

"August 18," Mama said as if that explained everything.

"Pleeeze, let me see!" I said.

She handed the paper to me. I turned it over and over. This wasn't a letter. It was a sheet covered with military mumbo jumbo that I couldn't read except for a date, August 18, and a place, Chu Lai.

"That's it?" I asked my mother. "That's all?"

I had been suffering from curiosity for months over that stupid letter, only to learn there was nothing interesting about it.

"Yes," she said. "That's it!"

"Then why did you wait? I don't get it. What is so special about August 18 that you wouldn't open it?"

"Because I didn't want to know. And you are being very rude."

"Didn't want to know what?" I said, trying my best not to be rude.

"I didn't want to know whether the day was . . . if your father had gotten . . . nothing, never mind—it's just another day. For a Marine's wife, it's just one more day." She looked tired as she took the letter from me and put it back in the envelope. Suddenly, a light bulb went off in my head. "I know what it is!" I exclaimed. "It's your anniversary! You and daddy were married on August 18! But so what's the big deal? You already know the day you married Daddy."

"Our wedding anniversary is a coincidence," Mama said as she left the room, and I heard her mutter under her breath, ". . . a very ironic coincidence."

In the end, the whole letter thing was the dumbest thing I'd heard of in my time on this planet. I had thought the envelope would reveal something exciting, something special. I had suffered through all that temptation and misery for nothing: A date, a date written on a piece of military paper. My curiosity had been driving me crazy for months over nothing. What a letdown!

Later though, after I had had time to go back and think it over, I couldn't help but wonder if Mama hadn't known all along that it was just a date written on a piece of paper from the military. In July, she had said that she knew what was in the envelope. And if she did, why didn't she want to open it? Why couldn't she open it. And if it wasn't because it was their wedding anniversary, if that was truly a coincidence, then what? Now I had something else to find out, and I needed to figure out how I was going to wheedle that something out of my mother. As it turned out, I didn't have to wheedle at all.

"Pat, Beebe, Scooter, come back here to your bedrooms, and let's go through all your clothes. We're going to try everything on. See what fits and what doesn't, what we need to buy for school, and what I need to mend."

"What's the hurry, Mama?" Pat asked. "We've never had to get our school clothes ready in the middle of the summer before."

"I have to do it now because . . . well, I need time to buy fabric and patterns and get started making school clothes for you girls because there are other things I have to do before school starts, and I want to get this out of the way. . . ."

Mama paused and frowned: "Because I said so. That's why."

Pat knew when to backtrack. "What are you planning on sewing, Mama?"

I found my sister's question reasonable, but Mama kept folding clothes as if she hadn't heard her. The lights in my brain began to flicker. Mama had packed the pink china two weeks ago. The kitchen was almost empty of food.

We were moving again.

Or were we? Maybe I was wrong. Maybe Mama was dusting the china cabinet and had taken the china out to do so. Maybe the pantry was empty because she hadn't felt like going to the grocery store in the stifling muggy August heat. And maybe I didn't want Mama to tell me what was going on because it was looking as if it might mean that we were getting ready to leave heaven. Which meant the other h-place was probably coming next.

I wasn't allowed to say that other word either.

CHAPTER 38

"TODAY WE'RE GOING TO FINISH all of this sewing," Mama declared. She was standing in the middle of the room, holding a pair of shorts she had picked from the floor, and looking around as if she couldn't figure out what to do next. "I don't want to pack anything we don't need. We'll see what can be let out a little bit and what you can wear a while longer. What fits will stay. What doesn't goes. I need all three of you to bring me everything that needs to be mended."

Pack? That word had come out of the blue.

"What do you mean *pack*, Mama?" I asked.

She ignored me. "Scott, we're giving all your clothes to Andy. Nothing fits; you've grown another foot."

She had said *pack*! Pack meant moving, just when our lives were perfect. Just like that. Moving. Again. I was stunned. Before I could ask, "Where to?"—Scooter started to holler.

"I don't growed another foot. I only got two feets like I always got."

"Don't say, 'don't growed.' Say, 'haven't grown.' "

"Haven't got no 'nother foot," Scooter said.

Mama sighed. "Don't say 'haven't got no.' Say 'haven't got any.' "

"Then why didja say I growed another one?"

"Say, 'I grew another one,' not 'I growed another one.' And *didja* is not a word," she added.

My mom is a nutcase about vocabulary, pronunciation, tense, and everything else about the English language. We have to answer the telephone, "To whom am I speaking?" No normal kid says whom to anywhom. But we do. Incorrect speech can delay your whole life in our house. A meal can grow cold while someone is splitting an infinitive, and everyone waits—indefinitely, while my mother's correction process goes on and on. Make the mistake of saying, *Gimme some of those potatoes* at the dinner table instead of *Would you please pass me the potatoes*, and a hungry kid might lose a pound or two before being allowed to start eating again.

My brother wasn't going to quit tormenting my mother about his feets, and she wasn't going to give up on correcting his English. I offered a truce. "You want me to help you, Scooter?" I asked. I would find out why we were packing later, when Mama wasn't in such a correcting-your-English fizz. Very mature of me. Very older sister behavior.

Pat was already sorting through her clothes. Wham, just like that. Pat takes life as it happens and adjusts around it. No questions asked. I don't understand her. Mama had delivered earth-shattering news, and Pat was calmly folding clothes and putting them into a box that Mama had set up in her room as if this was an everyday occurrence. Which, in our family, it was. I don't remember Pat ever asking why about anything. She had inherited Mama's lack of curiosity, and also like Mama, always seemed happy to go with the flow.

"Why do you think we're packing?" I whispered to my sister.

"Most probably because Daddy has orders," Pat whispered back.

"What makes you think that? Why would you say that? I thought Daddy was going to retire. Did you ask? Did you ask Mama if Daddy has orders?"

"No. What's the point?" Pat replied. "She won't say, and even if she did, it wouldn't change anything. It'd only waste time. Just do what Mama told you to do. Round up your stuff that needs to be mended. Wait and see what happens. You might learn something, Motormouth."

So much for being a mature big sister. Lately, Pat had taken to call-ing me Motormouth a lot—probably because I've had a lot more to say than usual. If only everyone knew all I kept to myself.

"You should say you're sorry for being rude to me and calling me a bad name," I told her.

Pat rolled her eyes. "You want me to remind you how many times you've been sent to your room to get humble? Huh?"

Then she went right on packing—as calm as if we packed every day, which, like I said, it sometimes seemed like we did, but this was differ-ent. I had settled in. I found the idea of leaving Beaufort unsettling.

"You two girls hush," Mama said. "Sort your clothes like I asked. I don't have time to listen to you quibble. Scooter, what are you doing?"

While Pat and I had been bickering, Scooter had begun to sort his toys—but, of course, not in any conventional way. One by one, he was tossing trucks and game pieces into the air trying to get them into the ceiling light fixture. Puzzle pieces, parts of toys. Educational toys were wasted on my brother. If a toy had parts and pieces, they became imagi-nary basketballs, baseballs, or footballs. Any and all toys were just some-thing to throw and hit something else with. Right now, the ceiling light fixture appeared to be his focus despite it being a fire hazard. But then, Scooter was a walking fire hazard himself. I could only imagine what he would be like in a few years. Lucky for him, he was so cheerful all the time that no one could stay mad at him for long—including Mama.

The secret to managing Scooter was redirection. Mama simply took the light fixture down and unscrewed the light bulb, removing the fire hazard and Scooter's impromptu goal. Then she put a wastebasket in-side a big packing crate on the floor. Before long, Scooter was picking up toys and throwing them at the wastebasket. And, I must say, hitting it every time. It was easier than throwing chicken necks to catch crabs. Scooter had a great arm. When he threw something, it was gonna go where he wanted it to go. Getting him to pack his toys was as simple as upending a basket into the packing crate. Mama is no dummy.

My brother was as oblivious to Mama's efforts as he'd been about the fire hazard his light-fixture antics posed. Dr. Phil had taught me that word, *oblivious*. "Totally unaware of the true circumstances of the moment," he said, "or of the day, or the year or . . ."—you get the picture. I did. Get the picture. My brother was oblivious.

"Two points, I's great!" Scooter suddenly hooted.

"That is 'I'm,' not 'I's,' " Mama said. Even in the middle of packing up our lives to go who knows where, Mama wasn't going to give up on instilling proper English in her son. You had to admire her optimism. Personally, I thought Scooter was hopeless.

As for me, I was growing more upset by the minute. I couldn't have been any sadder if she'd said that Scooter and I couldn't go crabbing any-more. A few minutes earlier, we'd been so happy. Now we were packing, which meant we were moving. It was as if the world had come to an end and nobody but me had noticed. I was five when we moved to Beaufort to the house on Laurel Bay, and now I was almost eight. I had been here almost half my life and had settled in as if we would never move again. And I had believed it. Why would the Marines make us move when Daddy had only six months left before he retired? Daddy had told me he was going to write the Marines a letter on August 19 so he could retire. On August 19, the day after August 18, which meant—what?

"Mama," I asked. "Where are we going? Why are we packing?"

Mama was still going through Scooter's clothes, tossing the ones that were too small for him into a laundry basket to set aside and give to Andy. She looked up for a moment and said: "Oklahoma—where Nana and Poppy live. We're moving home to Pryor Creek, Oklahoma."

"Why?"

"Because, we are."

"But why?" I asked. "What is there for Daddy to do in Oklahoma?"

"Shhh, hush, Bebee. You ask too many questions. Help your little brother—or better still, go try on your own clothes and figure out what doesn't fit anymore so we can give it away. Go on, now."

Subject closed. Finished. Done. I might as well go pack. I had a lot to think about anyway. I did not want to leave South Carolina. My life was perfect here. Mama had called Pryor home. Home was here in Laurel Bay, so how could Pryor, Oklahoma, be home?

And then I realized what all the packing might mean. Daddy was going to retire. That's why we were moving. I went from sad to glad in an instant. I have always been able to do that. I don't really have an intermediate mood.

I'm happy. Or I'm not.

I stayed happy clear through the next week while we did the work we always do when we're moving—cleaning, sorting, throwing things out, giving stuff away.

For six or seven days, at least, I was happy.

CHAPTER 39

MAMA WOULD NEVER LET the packers come in and just do what movers do. No, we had to follow Mama's system, and a moving company wasn't part of her system. That was a good thing, because when you used Mama's system, you could always find what you were looking for after you got to where you were going. If you let the movers pack your things, who knows what would turn up in which box. Some military families never found anything they needed for weeks after they moved. They had to borrow stuff from the neighbors, hoping the next box they opened would have what they had been looking for inside. Eventually, most of them would just give up and buy another one of whatever they hadn't been able to find and then end up with two whatevers. And sometimes, after a few moves, they ended up with three or four of everything.

Other families on base let the movers unpack their stuff. Not my Mama. She let the movers place the furniture inside the house, but the boxes were hers.

Daddy would ask, "Why do you go through this procedure every time we move? It seems like a lot of extra work. And besides, the movers won't insure it unless they pack it."

"I know, but they can pack it from my box into their box, and then I will label each of those boxes when they finish the transfer. That way I know exactly what's in every box. Otherwise, it'll be total confusion when we unpack because the movers just go from room to room and throw stuff into boxes."

Mama packed the boxes room by room, but in her own unique way. First, she packed everything in each room that we didn't need. Then a label went on the box. Toy room: Games, blocks, puzzles, Tinkertoys. Kitchen: Canning jars, pots and pans, dishes. Living room: Books, knick-knacks. The things we absolutely had to have to exist never got packed until the very last day. Little by little over those next few weeks, everything in our house vanished into boxes except for the essentials. Pat, Scooter, and I got to keep two or three of our favorite toys until the last box was ready to go—something to keep us from driving Mama crazy. Last packed, first opened. That was her system.

Mama always cleaned our rooms first and gave away everything we had accumulated that we no longer played with or wore. After all that was cleared out, she would start on the sewing room.

"If you want something mended, you had better tell me now or you are going to wear it for another month or two in whatever condition it is in," she would say. "If you need a button sewn on, bring it here or I'll have to safety-pin you together like tater-shed kids."

I rounded up all my clothes that needed mending and stacked them on the sewing machine. When Mama started talking about tater-shed kids, we knew things were serious. I didn't want to look like a tater-shed kid. We had been safety-pinned together before.

Tater-shed kids was an expression that Mama's mama, my grandma in Oklahoma, used. Gran was a farm woman who had always fed the people that the rails brought her way. Train tracks ran right by their farm. Hungry hobos, people down on their luck, sometimes entire families hopped the trains during the Great Depression—which I learned early wasn't a hole in the ground but something worse that no one has yet to clearly explain to me. Men, women, and children—people who had given up on life and were headed west to somewhere, anywhere but this dusty place—hopped trains because they had no money for a ticket.

They were fleeing hunger and looking for work. Gran said the mamas and daddys would hand their children up to the outstretched arms of those on board and hope they could jump onto the boxcar before the train pulled away from them. Poor people heading west passed the word along that you could get a free home-cooked meal at Gran and Pop's farm and sleep in the tater shed, where Gran and Pop stored potatoes and other root crops. Sometimes whole families would stay in the shed for a week or two before moving on. Some of the families moved from tater shed to tater shed clear across Oklahoma—hoppin' off and on trains, heading west, looking for a job, or sometimes going in the other direction because their hopes had run out. If they were going east, Gran said they were usually looking for family they had left behind—back before their dreams had died. Their children wore rags. That's where outgrown clothes ended up back then—on the tater-shed children.

In Beaufort, our old clothes ended up on whoever was the next size down in base housing. We weren't tater-shed kids; Mama wouldn't allow it. We always had a place to sleep and our daddy always had a job. We were more like upscale migrants who wore passed-around hand-me-downs. Being a tater-shed family meant you had reached the bottom of the barrel: poor folk with nowhere else to go.

When we started packing for a move, our house always became a popular place. Every kid in Laurel Bay spent some time hanging around and going through our trash hunting for treasure. Each afternoon, Mama set a big box on the driveway near the street, and neighbors checked the box every so often to see what we were tossing out. That was how we did it in the military. You packed what you needed, and the rest went into your box of giveaways, set out on the driveway for everyone to go through. After a couple of years, people sometimes ended up reclaiming their own stuff after it had vanished into someone else's stuff during an earlier move only to be set out by the road again. Stuff vanished, showed up, and moved but seldom was thrown away.

"Are you really throwing those curtains out?" Jeanette called to Mama through our kitchen door. "I want to be sure before I take them."

"Take them! I'll be glad if you can use them. I've recut them three times and never want to see them again. They didn't fit a single window when we moved here, but I held onto them because you never know. But where we're going, I'm going to start all over again on curtains. When we get where we're going, I'm going to make formal drapes. That fit. I'm hoping this is our last move—ever."

If I had overheard right, Mama was going to throw out all the old drapes and start from scratch. Even I knew what that meant: Daddy was retiring!

This would be our last move.

Hallelujah, thank you Jesus! as our beloved Mrs. Washington liked to say. Mrs. Washington was our housekeeper and a dear friend. She loved us and we loved her. And when Mama and Daddy had to be gone in the evenings, it was Mrs. Washington who took us home with her to stay the night. And if it was a Saturday night, we got to go to church the next morning with her and her husband, Al. Everyone at their church loved to sing, and some folks would get so excited about Jesus and his daddy that sometimes they would clap and shout, *Amen* or *Hallelujah* or *Praise the Lord*! Mrs. Washington's church was a lot more fun than ours. The only bad part was that everyone stared at us.

I think because we were so white.

CHAPTER 40

A DAY OR TWO AFTER WE HAD started packing, I began to have some doubts. Doubts about why we were moving. I could not get Mama to say that Daddy was going to retire. That was the first thing. Then I had learned we were moving on the same day as the day in the letter, the one Daddy had sent to Mama that neither one ever mentioned. And then I thought about how quickly Daddy had promised me that before the summer was over, sometime in late August, we would go to Oklahoma and play in Saline Creek and catch frogs. He had promised a little too fast. Usually a kid has to beg for a while to get anything good, and I had barely had to beg at all. That meant Daddy already knew we were going to Oklahoma in August when he promised me. He *knew*. And Mama knew too, but for some reason, she didn't want to talk about it to me, to Daddy, or to anyone else.

I grew restless trying to figure out what it all meant. I wandered through our house, touching all the familiar things in the rooms. The old black Naugahyde sectional sofa—torn on one corner where it had hit the pavement after falling off the pickup Daddy had borrowed, right smack in the middle of Highway 1 in Virginia. We had been moving ourselves closer to Quantico, closer to base. The sofa sat in the middle of the highway and stopped traffic for a while until Daddy and Mama could get it back onto the pickup.

"Strap it on the truck, and I'll deal with that torn spot later," Mama had said. "I can cover the hole with an afghan."

I touched the cherry end table that Mama and I had bought on one of our looking days. One drawer in front and a crack down the middle of the top. Mama had taken it to be repaired by a local handyman. The man must have known what he was doing, because now the crack was visible only on the bottom when you turned the table over. "Anybody that would look under that table probably wouldn't be a guest in my house anyway," Mama had said upon its return.

The room I shared with Pat had a pair of hand-carved alabaster lamps that we had found in Alexandria, Virginia. The bases of the lamps were angels leaning on a lamppost entwined with grapevines. When Mama bought the lamps, she said the angels would watch over her two girls because Jesus and his angels were busy watching over Amy.

"What about Scooter? Why didn't you buy an angel lamp for his room?" I had asked her at the time. "Doesn't he need an angel too?"

"I don't think the angels would know what to do with Scooter," Mama had said.

I slowly looked around my room. Pat and I had the coolest room of any of the girls we knew. There were matching twin trundle beds with rattan headboards that Mama had found for us so we could pull out the trundles and have our friends over for slumber parties. There were matching bright orange-and-yellow floral quilted bedspreads that she had made to fit the twin beds, with matching scalloped valances over the windows.

I wandered into the dining room, opened the silver chest, took out the old butter knife, and turned it over, looking for the permanently notched, blackened spot from when I had stuck it in the light socket. I felt so confused. I was glad we were going to see our grandparents in Oklahoma, so why was I so miserable?

One by one, I touched the old treasures that Mama and I had bought so long ago, back when we would get in the car every morning and take off for anywhere, looking. Back when I felt as if I was her only child, back when Pat was in kindergarten, and Daddy was learning to speak French in junior school, Amy was in General Lee's front yard, and Scooter was still on the shelf at the PX.

I picked up one of the sterling forks and could almost hear Mama saying, "Look, Beebe! Somebody is breaking up their family's home, and no one wants this silver; nobody wants to shine it anymore. It's so sad. Think of all the people who ate supper with these beautiful knives and forks. Someone in their family must have loved pretty things. What do you think? Should we buy them? Save them from being melted down?" In my mind's eye, I could see her standing in front of the old two-story house with the "Estate Sale" sign in the front yard that day.

Silver knives, forks, and spoons. They were beautiful. There was a meat fork that had a clamp and a sterling handle. There were serving spoons and a bunch of other big serving pieces, all heavy and crusted with floral engraving. "Stieff repousse," Mama had whispered to me. "Maybe they don't know what they have? I think we absolutely have to buy them. I have fifteen dollars. Let's see what we can dig out of the car seats."

We had returned to the car and dug through school papers, smashed paper cups, paper clips, and chewing-gum wrappers beneath the seats. We came up with four dollars and fifty-seven cents in change. "I've got a quarter you can have," I had told Mama. "Daddy gave it to me. How much does that make?"

"You tell me, Beebe. My fifteen. Four dollars and fifty-seven cents we found under the car seat. And your twenty-five cents. How much is that?" Mama was always giving me math problems like that to solve. She said doing math was good for my brain.

"I can do the fifteen and the four. That's sixteen, seventeen, eighteen, nineteen. But I can't do the fifty-seven and the twenty-five in my head. It's more than nineteen dollars, but closer to twenty," I'd said. "Do you think it will be enough?"

"*Fantabulous.* You have your daddy's brain and my optimism, a perfectly outstanding combination. Let's use our optimism and see if the man will let us have it all for twenty dollars minus a few cents."

And the man did! We took the silver home, shined all the pieces, and ate dinner with them every night after that until Daddy changed his first name to Lieutenant Colonel and bought Mama a full set of Gorham La Scala with all the serving pieces. After that, we used the old repousse set every morning for breakfast. I grew up thinking that everybody ate their Cheerios with sterling silver spoons.

"If I had some real money, I'd buy every pretty thing I could get my hands on," Mama once told me. "Pretty never goes out of date, and someday these families will be very sorry that they let their treasures go. Such beautiful things. Such craftsmanship. Made to last generations."

Anything that had taken expert hands to create, those were the things that always caught her eye. "See how the drawers of this chest are held together with dovetails, and each dovetail is a little different because it is handmade. I bet some man made this for his family. Look how the drawer fronts are inlaid with burled walnut and the handles are solid brass." I learned a lot about old stuff that year from Mama. She called our finds antiques, and said it would ruin me when I grew up because once you've seen how the best is constructed, you would rather do without than buy something cheap and ugly that's glued together.

She considered what we found to be treasure. She would wonder out loud about the stories behind each piece—about the craftsman who had made them, about the family who had originally owned them but was now having to let them go. Some days we would sneak out of the house early in the morning before the others were awake, flashlights in hand. We'd head for the yards of the old mansions, dig through tables piled high with crystal, china, Spode, Delft, Dresden, Waterford . . .

"Oh, if I only had some *real money*," Mama would say.

I wasn't sure what the difference between *money* and *real money* was, but from the way Mama said it, we didn't have any of the real kind.

For me, the best part of those early morning treks was wandering around in the dark with a flashlight in my hand with my mother.

"Beebe, quit clicking that flashlight off and on and shine it over here—I think I've found something!" Mama would say.

And then away we would go again—on the hunt for more treasure.

As I wandered through our house, touching those beautiful old things and remembering, I ached with a feeling I could not put into words.

CHAPTER 41

THE MOVERS FINALLY CAME. Mama explained her system to them. They did what Mama said, and she gave them sweet tea and cookies. Our stuff had already been packed away and separated into four stacks in the living and dining rooms. One stack was going into storage. The second stack was going with us in the car to Oklahoma. The third, mostly furniture, linens, and kitchen things, was going on the moving van to our new house in Oklahoma. The last group of boxes was all Daddy's stuff. They were marked: "Ken."

"Mama," I asked her, "are you and Daddy mad at each other?"

"Now why would you think something silly like that?" she asked.

"Because all of Daddy's stuff is stacked by itself," I pointed out. "Where are the boxes marked 'Ken' going? Isn't he going with us?"

"Well, he is, but he has to go somewhere with his friends for a little while after that," she said.

"What friends? Where? Is he going back to Puerto Rico? Why?"

Mama held up a hand like a crossing guard. "I do not know the answers to any of that. He'll be gone as long as it takes."

I couldn't resist one more try: "How long will *as long as it takes* be?"

"Beebe, you ask too many questions. Enough!"

Mama was finished talking to me, but her abrupt dismissal had made me mad. "Dr. Phil calls me by my real name. He always calls me, *Rebecca*. He treats me like I am halfway intelligent and answers my questions. You treat me like a baby and call me Beebe and never tell me anything. I am not a baby!"

"Okay, okay, you're right," Mama said to my surprise. "You are growing up. I will call you Becky from now on. No more Beebe. Now, Becky, excuse me. I'm too busy to answer any more questions."

<hr/>

I waited at the end of the driveway for a long time that evening. Daddy was late. When he finally pulled into the drive, my first words to him were, "You promised you would take me to Saline Creek and catch frogs this August. You promised!"

"What's going on, Punkin?" he said. "What are you upset about? I'm going to take you to the creek to catch critters in August. I told you I would, and I'm a man of my word. What would make you think I have changed my mind?"

"Your stuff isn't going in the van with ours. You aren't going to Oklahoma with us."

"Yes, I am—we're all going in the car together. I'm going to drive us to Oklahoma, and we're going to roller-skate and go to Saline Creek and catch crawdads and snails and wade in the water."

"And then what, Daddy? What's going to happen then? Why isn't your stuff coming with ours? Where is all your stuff going? I might be a little kid, but I know something's going on. Did you get orders? Or are you retiring? Why are we going to Oklahoma? Mama says I ask too many questions and she won't tell me what's going on."

"Well, Punkin', after I learn how to roller-skate, and after we go to the creek and catch tadpoles, and after we do everything else that you wanted to do, then after a while . . . well, I have one more job to do before I can retire and grow a beard. What kind of beard do you think I should grow? How about a long pointed one?" He was trying to change the subject, but I wasn't having it.

"What is this one more job?" I asked. "How many days will it take? Where is it? Nobody tells me anything and I don't know why! I finished first grade and I'm big enough to know stuff. And I don't want to talk about beards. Every time I ask you an important question, you start talking about beards or rookies or tigers or something. Mama hates beards. You'll get food in it, and it will be sticky like Scooter's hair after a supper with gravy."

"Well, hmmm, that's a lot of questions. Did your mother say you and I couldn't go to Saline Creek?"

"No, she didn't, but she won't tell me anything. I have to figure everything out by myself. I saw your boxes over to one side—away from the ones going to Oklahoma. And Mama told the movers not to pack or load them. Why?"

"Hmmm, I guess I'll have to take a look at the boxes later and see if I can figure that out," Daddy said. "Now, where's my pipe? And why don't you go get me the newspaper? I need to unwind for a little while before we eat. What's for supper?"

"Daddy, I want to know! When can you write your letter to retire?"

"Well, now, let me see. I guess that would be August 19," he said.

"Do you have orders? What is the one more job you are going to do? What day is on your orders to go do one more job?"

"Well, I guess that would be August 18."

I was on a roll, and quickly decided now was the time to go through my questions one by one, starting with the one that had been bothering me the most. "If you get orders first, Daddy, if you get those orders before you can ask to retire, can you still retire?"

"Well, yes and no," he said. "If you get orders before the day that you can ask to retire, the government can send you somewhere to serve one more year—sometimes on a carrier, sometimes overseas, sometimes to some other duty station. I missed the retirement boat by one day because my orders are dated August 18. And since I can't submit my retirement letter until August 19, I have to serve another year instead of six more months."

It was not the answer I had wanted, but it was an answer. Things were starting to make some sense.

"The good news, Punkin, is then I can retire—and I will retire. I promise! I just can't do it now because the Marine Corps needs me to do one last job. It's a hard one that not many Marines know how to do because they haven't ever seen the elephant. Now where's your mother?"

With that, he picked me up, threw me over his shoulder, and headed inside to the kitchen, all the while tickling my feet and yelling, "What's for supper? I have a curious little girl here who wants her supper!"

By the time he put me down, I had forgotten all about his stuff being in a different stack. I was laughing so hard I couldn't have asked another question even if I had wanted to—and so was my daddy.

Better to laugh than to cry. I knew where he was going, and now I knew why that date in the letter Daddy wrote to Mama was so important. He had mailed her the letter because Mama didn't want to know about his orders. That's why Mama didn't want to open it. She didn't want to know whether Daddy had orders or whether he was going to retire without another deployment. She didn't want to know one way or another, not one day before she absolutely had to know. That way, she could spend the whole summer pretending the letter meant he was retiring. And if he had orders, she didn't want to know where the Marine Corps was sending him. Like I said before, my mother has no curiosity. "It's better to live one day at a time," she would always say.

I'm no Einstein, but some things even a little kid can figure out. And it didn't have anything to do with elephants or flying tigers. That much I knew for sure. I knew where my daddy was going.

After supper was over and my father was settled in his chair with the newspaper, I crawled up on his lap. "Daddy, can I ask you one last question, and will you give me a real answer?"

"Okay, if you promise me this is the last one."

"Two."

"Okay, two. But I swear, that's it. No more."

"Will you come home someday? And when you do, will you stay?"

"I promise you this, Punkin, God willing, I'll come home. God willing, I'll never leave home again. God willing . . ."

That night after I put on my pajamas, I got on my knees and said my prayers without being reminded. I don't remember whether I called

God Jehovah or Dear Heavenly Father. I don't think God cares much either way. But I do remember what I said:

> *I need for you to listen to me very carefully. I have not done any sins in a long time, so I figure I have plenty of grace stored up wherever you keep it.*
>
> *I need for you to take care of my daddy when I can't see him anymore, when he gets to where he is going. I think you and I already know where that is, even if nobody will tell me.*

My breath caught in my throat.

> *Would you get him some special angel wings for his plane too? And anything else you have up there that he could use to keep him safe. I guess that's it. Thank you. Amen.*

I crawled into my bed and pulled the covers over my head, as a parade of tigers and rookies and gasoline and elephants marched through my thoughts. Tears started and I couldn't stop them. My pink heart was broken and I didn't know how to fix it.

I don't know how Mama knew what I was feeling, but she must have sensed something was wrong because before my tears could dry, she had slipped into my room, crawled into bed with me, and softly begun to sing a song from church.

> *Leaning on the everlasting arms . . .*
> *. . . what have I to fear . . .*

I fell asleep somewhere after *what have I to fear.*

I never had to be reminded to say my prayers again after that night. Saying my prayers when I went to bed became part of me, like breathing comes when you are born.

CHAPTER 42

"ARE WE CLEAR ABOUT WHICH things go on the van?" Mama asked the movers. "We got it, Lady—stuff in the living room goes on the van, stuff in the dining room don't." "Right!" my mother said. "The things in the dining room are suitcases and the things we're taking to Oklahoma with us. All of that is going in our car. Please tell your men to stay out of the dining room, and it shouldn't be a problem. You've already loaded all the furniture. Do you have any idea how much longer you'll be before you're finished?"

"Cuppla' hours, at least."

"Okay, so that means you should still be here when I get back. I won't be gone that long. I left a pitcher of iced tea on the counter in the kitchen for you and your men."

" 'Preciate that, Lady," the mover man replied.

"You won't forget to tell your men about the things in the dining room?" Mama asked.

"I gotcha, Lady. I gotcha. I'll tell 'em."

Mama turned to me, "Beebe, you run next-door to the Golfeders'. I have to go get your father."

"Why can't I go with you?"

"Because if Pat comes home, I don't want her to be by herself while the movers are here. She's gone to a friend's house to play, and I want someone to be watching for her in case she gets home before I do. Scooter is at the sitter's, so you don't need to worry about him. I'll pick him up on the way home."

"Why?"

"Why what?"

"Why are you going to get Daddy?"

"Your father doesn't have a car. He sold his, so we only have to mess with one car on the drive to Oklahoma—we're only going to need one car after that anyway."

"Why?"

"Why what?"

"Why won't we need two cars? Who won't need one? You? Daddy?"

"Your father . . . because he . . ."

"Why doesn't Daddy need a car?"

"Because he doesn't need one. *Because*, that's why."

"How's he going to get to work?"

I thought my question reasonable, but could tell by the way Mama was now eyeing me that she did not agree. Once again, I had exceeded my limit on asking questions. Once again. Mama put her hands on her hips—never a good sign.

"You ask too many questions, Beebe," Mama said. "Now, git! Go on over to Jeanette's and play with Andy until I get back—and watch for Pat."

"You said you wouldn't call me Beebe anymore, and what if I don't want to play with Andy?"

"Okay, then, Miss Becky, go on over to Jeanette's, and *don't* play with Andy. Just git—do you hear me?"

I did, but I was not happy about it. "*Git's* not a word!" I yelled at her retreating back. I had to get that in. My mother turned around and gave me the look before grabbing her purse and car keys, waving goodbye, and heading out the door. Defeated, I wandered over to Andy's house and found him in the front yard. He was watching the movers carry things out of our house and load them onto the moving van.

"That truck's a monster!" Andy said. "It's swallowing your furniture. I betcha you never see any of it ever again."

"Shut up, Andy. You talk too much," I said.

"Don't either!"

"Do!"

"Anyway, you didn't supposed to say shut up to people," Andy said.

"*You aren't supposed to say.* Not *didn't supposed to say.* And I wouldn't have to say shut up if you didn't talk too much."

"Don't either!"

I heaved a sigh. This exchange had forever written all over it. "Okay, okay, you win. Whatever you say."

Andy grinned; he didn't win often. Satisfied now with the outcome of our exchange, he made a peace offering. "Let's go look at Dad's brain jars 'cause it may be the last time you ever get to see a real brain. I heard they don't have any brains in Oklahoma."

Andy and I spent some time looking at the brains until his mother called us into the kitchen, told us we surely had better things to do with our time than look at jars full of brains, and made each of us a Coke float. "We're going to miss you and your family, Becky. I wonder if we will ever see each other again?" she said.

It would have been better if she hadn't said anything, or if she hadn't been so nice, or if she had told us we were wasting our time looking at brains again instead of talking about us not ever seeing each other again. I didn't want to think about not seeing people again. Even Andy. I was already hurting somewhere inside, and once again, I didn't know how to fix it.

CHAPTER 43

"WHERE ARE OUR SUITCASES? Where are all the boxes that were in the dining room?" Mama was wandering through our empty house looking confused. "Where are the movers? And where is the moving van?"

"I don't know, Mama. I went over to Andy's like you told me."

"The suitcases. They were in the dining room when I left. I told the man . . . Oh, surely he didn't. Becky, when did the men leave?"

"I don't know, Mama. They loaded a bunch of boxes, smashed the garbage cans flat, and tied them on the back of the truck. Then they left."

"Smashed the garbage cans? Did you say they smashed the garbage cans?" Mama said.

"Yep. One guy said—"

"Man, not guy. And *yes*, not *yep*."

I tried again. "One *man* said, 'There ain't no room for them cans. They's too big,' and the other man said, 'Smash 'em and strap 'em on the back of the truck.' Then he told me to tell you to take it out of the 'surance. And he was the one who used *ain't* and *'em*. Not me."

"He smashed the metal trash cans?"

"Yep—smashed them flat and tied them on the back of the truck."

"Did you see where he put the boxes that were in the dining room?"

"Nope, me and Andy were looking at brains while they were finishing up loading."

"Nope? Did you say *nope*? Did you say *me and Andy*, or did you say *Andy and I*?"

"Yes, I mean 'no ma'am,' not nope. Andy and I were looking at Dr. Phil's brains."

My father had come in while Mama was questioning me. He was in full dress uniform, ready for his change of command ceremony. Medals, sword, ribbons, and red stripes down his trouser legs. He had silver leaves on his shoulders and wings on his chest. He looked so handsome, almost royal, like a king.

"You look pretty, Daddy," I said. "I like your red stripes."

"Punkin, that's just what I was aiming for, pretty. Thank you. I'll tell my friends you said so; they'll like that." He winked at Mama. "I assume you girls packed my traveling clothes in the suitcases. Am I right that those are the suitcases that have vanished?"

"I don't believe this," my mother said.

"Guess that means when the ceremony is over, I'll be driving to Oklahoma in my dress blues. We'll let all the people along the way from South Carolina to Oklahoma see how pretty I am," he said.

"If you don't mind, we'll deal with that later," my mother said. "I have a much bigger problem on my hands that I have to solve right now. Everything I was going to wear to the goodbye luncheon the ladies are giving for me is in one of those missing suitcases. And I only have one hour to get to town and buy shoes, a dress, makeup, and jewelry. Oh, my stars, I'm going to have to use a credit card! I swore I would never charge anything again in my life. I hate owing money. How will I ever get all of this paid for after you're . . . you know."

"Just wear what you have on," Daddy told her. "You look pretty good in those denim cutoffs, halter, and sandals. No, you look better than pretty good. As a matter of fact . . ."

"Ken, hush—don't you start with me!" Mama said.

"Okay, okay, I hear you—but if you should change your mind, you know where to find me. I think you should go to the luncheon dressed in shorts and that halter top. Everyone there would get a kick out of you showing up in cutoffs. Just one more military moving story. They all have a bucketful of moving stories themselves. And don't worry about money. I got paid."

"There is absolutely no way I am going to a fancy luncheon looking like this," my mother told him, "and you know it. Especially when it's in my honor!"

Daddy shrugged. "Well, look on the bright side. Next week, this will be just one more funny story to go with all the other funny stories from our life in the military."

My mother still wasn't smiling. "It's not funny! I don't believe this! They took everything—our bags, the suitcases with all of our clothes. Everything I put in the dining room is gone. No, I do believe this. I have one hour to get ready for the luncheon, and then we have two hours to get ready for the change of command ceremony, and your children have nothing to wear."

No one said a word. We could tell Mama was working her way through the options.

"So let me think. Let me think," she said. "I don't have time to shop for all of us, so while you are waiting for me to get back, why don't you see if you can find an empty box you can use for a table. You and Beebe—I'm sorry, *Becky*—can play cribbage after she gets back from finding herself some clothes. I left your cribbage board on the kitchen counter—if the movers didn't haul that away too. Beebe, you have to find something to wear."

"*Becky!*" I said.

My mother glared at me. "Whatever," she said.

Daddy intervened before things went south. "Okay, sounds like a plan," he said. "I'm going to need a new partner soon anyway. You want to learn to play cribbage, Punkin? You know how to peg? You have to add numbers up to make a total of fifteen if you want to learn to peg and to play cribbage."

"Of course, Daddy, I can add to fifteen. I'm going into the second grade! I know all my adding numbers. When my class was learning one-sies and twosies, I was so bored I learned how to add up all the rest. I know how to add to fifteen—seven and eight, six and nine, and a bunch of other little numbers you can put together to make fifteen."

Daddy nodded. "Do you know the rules?"

"I know how. I've watched you and Dr. Phil."

"Okay, then you can be my partner," Daddy said.

"Beebe—excuse me—*Becky*," my mother said, "before you start playing cribbage, I want you to run down the street, knock on doors, and tell them what's happened. Explain that you don't have any clothes for the ceremony. Borrow something. I'll call Pat. She can borrow a dress at her friend's house and wear it home. I have to hurry to get to town. What else could happen? Good grief! One more day in the life of . . ."

Suddenly she looked around. "Where's my purse? Oh! It's in my hand! Thank goodness I took it with me or I'm sure those movers would have packed that too." She wasn't talking to me anymore; she was talking to herself. You could see her brain buzzing a hundred miles an hour and the wheels smoking.

"Jeanette took some of Scooter's old clothes for Andy. Go check with her and see if she took anything that your brother can still wear. My stars, what else could go wrong? You get yourself together as best you can, and I'll be back as soon as I can."

I had to knock on only three doors before I had shoes, anklets, and a dress—even a barrette for my hair that matched the dress. "Take them," one of our neighbors down the street insisted. "My little girl has outgrown them anyway. What happened?"

"The movers took our suitcases," I explained. "And we have to go to some ceremony, the changing of . . . the something. And we don't have anything to wear."

"Well, when you get back from the ceremony, tell your mama to come see me. I'll have some things ready for her. The dentist gave me some tubes of toothpaste, new toothbrushes. Bet I have extras of most anything you might need. Tell her no need to buy anything. I'll make a few calls. I know everyone on the street will want to pitch in. Okay?"

"Thank you!" I said.

I knew the first thing Mama would ask when she saw me next was if I had said thank you. I ran all the way home, put on my borrowed clothes, and went looking for a hairbrush. I couldn't find one, of course, because they were all in one of the suitcases the movers had taken.

"I'll be back to play cribbage in a minute," I told Daddy.

"I don't have anywhere to go," he said. "I'll deal and be waiting for you right here."

I went next-door and asked Jeanette if she would please brush my hair and help me fix the barrette.

"Well, Becky, it's a good thing some of your hair has grown back since you gave yourself that haircut or there wouldn't be anything to brush," Jeanette said with a chuckle as she worked the hairbrush through my hair. "You have pretty hair, you know. It's the color of toasted almonds and nice and thick. I do hope you never try to cut it yourself again. Last time, you ended up looking like you had run into a lawn mower. Next time you need a haircut—please go to the beauty shop!"

I tried not to squirm as she worked the brush through a tangle. "Don't worry—Mama will cut it for me next time. She does Daddy and Scooter's crew cuts. She says girl hair takes more time and is harder to do, but I can't imagine Mama spending money at a beauty shop when she could cut my hair herself for free."

"Now, Becky, your mom might take you," Jeanette said. "I wish I had a little girl I could take to the beauty shop."

"You can get you one at the PX," I told her.

"Really!" She laughed. "What section?"

I explained how we had gotten my brother.

"Well, now, that's very interesting," Jeanette said. "I will check that out. I certainly will. Sounds much easier than . . . In fact, if you'll send me your address when you get to Oklahoma, I'll be sure to write and let you know when Phil and I get our little girl from the PX and what we name her! Or do they come already named from the PX?"

"I don't know about that part," I told her, "because no one seems to know exactly what my brother's name is. Everyone calls him something different. Scooter or Scotty. Daddy calls him Sam. You'll have to ask my mother about the baby names."

"You can be sure I'll ask your mom all about that." Jeanette had a big grin on her face. I didn't get what was so funny.

"I have to go home and play cribbage with my dad," I told her. "Thank you for fixing my hair. Oh, I almost forgot. Mama said I'm supposed to get something for my brother to wear."

"Certainly, give me a minute," Jeanette said. "I put the hand-me-downs your mother gave me in Andy's closet in a bag. Andy has to grow a little bit before they'll fit him anyway. I'll find something for Scooter and bring it over."

When I got home, my father was still sitting on the cardboard box in his dress blues, patiently waiting for me.

"Well, you look nice!" he said. "How about getting that cribbage board, and we'll see if someone as pretty as you can beat me."

He won the first game; I won the second and third.

"Did you let me win?" I asked him.

"Now does that sound like something a Marine would do? Let someone else win? Why would I do something like that?"

When Mama returned from picking up Scooter and Pat, she was wearing a new red dress and a necklace made of pearls with sparkle beads set between the pearls and earrings to match. Dangling earrings that moved when she turned her head. Open-toed shoes made of material so clear that you could see through it and count her toes, with red dots scattered across the top of the shoes. Cool. She was always so cool. Me? Well, regardless of what Daddy had just said, I knew I would probably never make it all the way to bathed, dressed, shoes on, and hair done all at the same time.

My sister looked me up and down and exclaimed, "Good grief, Becky, you have a dress on! You look like a girl for a change. Maybe there's hope for you yet—if you'll quit cutting your own hair."

CHAPTER 44

ALL OF US MADE IT TO the ceremony. Nothing we had on fit exactly right, but Mama declared us presentable. Although she could not resist reminding us not to act like tater-shed kids—though by *us*, she meant me and Scooter.

"Try to act civilized," she told Scooter. "Becky, just this once, please, no questions." I overheard my mother whisper to my sister, "Pat, see if you can keep your little brother and sister from getting dirty for one hour. I would appreciate it if you could also keep them from embarrassing your father and me."

"Impossible," Pat replied.

"I know, but would you please try?"

"I'll do the best I can," Pat said, "but there isn't much to work with."

Even in our borrowed clothes, I thought we looked pretty good, but Daddy in his uniform and Mama in her new red dress were spectacular. They looked so different than they did at home. Without thinking, I reached out my hand and touched my mother to make sure she was real.

She turned to look at me. "Are your hands clean?" she asked.

Yep, she was real. Then she took my offending hand and held it in hers, softly, so if I wanted to slip loose, I could. I didn't. These two beautiful people were my parents, and I was overcome with a feeling I could not describe.

The only thing I can think of that compares to a changing of command ceremony would be a big parade I once saw on television of the Marines coming down Pennsylvania Avenue in Washington, D.C. And just like in that parade, these Marines were all in dress uniform and marching in perfect time as one of them counted cadence. I was so close that I could hear the clanking of their swords when they drew them from their scabbards. Their uniforms were covered with ribbons in every color of the rainbow—just like in the movies. They started marching together; they stopped together. Every movement they made, they made together. Swords, gold, silver, everyone in perfect step. Unlike the parade on TV, in this one my father was the center of attention.

And then it was over.

Afterward, everyone wanted to speak to him. I heard them congratulating him and saw them saluting him. I wasn't sure I knew this person who had marched in the ceremony. He was so serious, so dignified.

"Honor serving under you, Sir," one man said.

"Best year of my life, Sir," another added.

A crowd was gathering around my father, saying their goodbyes.

"Enough, enough, you have a new commander now. Do him proud," my father said.

"Yes, Sir, we will!" they all replied.

"I'll be seeing you soon," one of the young men said.

"I hope not!" Daddy replied. "Ask for assignment to Cherry Point or El Toro."

"You know, Sir, with all due respect, I want to go to—"

My daddy interrupted him before the Marine could finish. "Okay, okay, I hear you. You want to be a hero. Just don't ask for it. Try to get a year stateside, more flight time if you can before . . . but if it happens, let me know when you get there . . . I might be able to get you into my . . ." I didn't hear the rest.

Finally, Mama broke away from the women who were saying their goodbyes and promising to write—knowing they probably wouldn't, knowing they likely would never see each other again either. My father gave the men a final salute—and we left.

"Best time in the Corps I've ever spent, finest year of my life," my father said as we got in the car to leave.

"Giving it up to someone else, changing command . . . all those young men," my mother reached over and took my father's hand. "They couldn't have had a better teacher."

"How would you know?" My daddy laughed. "You've never even seen me fly, as I recall! You always said that was just a rumor."

"Let's say I hear things." Mama smiled at him. "Wives talk, you know. And so do the men, for that matter."

"Well, most Marines only dream of having a squadron. I got to live it. It doesn't get any better than that; I'm going to miss it. And yes, it's hard to give it up, but I'm sure I'll see some of them again before the year is up. And then I'll find out if they learned what they were supposed to learn. I hope to God they did."

"You're not done yet. There might be another squadron before this is over," Mama told him.

"Yes, but it won't be the same. People in squadrons where I'm going are going to get—" he hesitated and looked over his shoulder at me and Pat and Scooter in the back seat. And then said, "You know, I could stay in the Corps for another ten years, but what would be the point. After this next year, my career would only be paper and more paper at the Pentagon. I'm not going to the Pentagon. I hate paper. I've had two squadrons and maybe there will be a third. Most Marine aviators don't even get one."

"What other squadron?" I piped up.

No one answered me. My parents were talking to each other, and I might as well have been on the moon.

"I had some of these rookies for the entire year," Daddy told her, "but then they'd get orders and be gone. All I could do was pray that they had learned enough to . . . they're so young, and there's never enough time, never enough gasoline for them to learn everything they needed to learn before they're transferred, before they got orders to . . ." I had heard my parents talking about something that was "none of your business" before, so I knew there was no use asking them what they were talking about. I knew what they would say: "You are a nosy little critter."

When we arrived back home, Dr. Phil, Jeanette, and Andy walked over to our house to say their goodbyes, and I set Andy straight on a couple of matters. "My daddy's sword has a real ivory hilt," I told him. "He got it before anyone knew the elephants were going 'stinct."

"*Extinct*, Idgit" my sister whispered in my ear, saving me the embarrassment of Andy overhearing her correct me. Sometimes older sisters surprise you with unexpected kindness.

"Huh-uh, no, he duddn't. That's unlegal!" Andy shouted.

"Uh-huh," I countered. "My daddy has an ivory hilt on his sword."

"Duddn't!"

"Does!" I retorted.

I was going to miss Dr. Phil and his family, and having an argument with Andy was as good a way as any to say goodbye, especially when I knew I was right. Daddy had told me once that only old timers had ivory hilts on their swords. The ivory was a thing of the past, like ivory piano keys, gone forever. "Good riddance too, because elephants look pretty funny without their teeth," Daddy had said.

"Kennn . . .," my mother had interrupted in the voice she always uses when she wants Daddy to hush.

"Tusks," I corrected him.

"Right, tusks," Daddy said. "Shame they couldn't have made the sword hilts out of kid tusks, since kids lose all their tusks anyway. The tooth fairy could have donated all those kid tusks to the Marines to make sword hilts."

"Teeth, Daddy," I told him. "Kids have teeth, not tusks."

"Teeth, tusks, all I can say is it's a good thing they invented something else."

"Is that why you say your men have never seen the elephant?" I asked him. "Because they don't have ivory hilts on their swords?"

"Not exactly, Punkin, what I meant was . . ."

"I mean it," my mother said, "that's enough nonsense!"

CHAPTER 45

Pryor, Oklahoma
2010

"AS YOU MAY REMEMBER, your father took a month's leave before he left," Mama said. "There was so much to do in the new house in Oklahoma—unpacking, hanging drapes, painting walls. It was the first house we had ever owned, and your father didn't want to leave me with a lot of unfinished work to do. We were so busy those last few weeks. You children had to be enrolled in school. Such an awful lot to do."

"We painted my new room yellow," I said. "I remember helping you paint."

"Well, yes, I guess you could call it that," Mama said. "You spilled a gallon of yellow paint, as I recall, and we had to replace the carpet in your bedroom."

"I thought I was helping!" I couldn't keep from laughing as I remembered the mess the spilled paint had made.

"Sure, laugh," my mother said. "Now, it's funny. Back then, I could have strangled you. When I showed your father what had happened, he looked at the mess and just started ripping the carpet out. Told me to go to town, get some more paint, and order new carpet—but to be sure I told them to wait to deliver the carpet until we finished painting."

"I remember the part when you and I went to town to buy the new carpet. Do you remember telling me on the way to town that it would be okay with you if I spilled paint all over the house—so we could replace all the carpet?"

"Oh, no, surely not! I don't remember saying that," my mother said with a laugh. "I do remember what your father told you. You were so upset about the carpet and kept telling him how sorry you were about spilling the paint. You were worried about what it would cost to repaint and replace the carpet. Your father just looked at you and said, 'It's just carpet, Punkin, it can be replaced. Little girls can't. However, you and your mother might want to get some carpet that's yellow, just in case.' Your face went from cloudy to sunshine in an instant. Your father never seemed to get upset about things that got broken or needed to be replaced; he always said, 'It's just money.' "

" 'Of which we don't have any extra,' you would reply."

Mama nodded. "And your father would say, 'It will all work out.' "

"And somehow it always did," I said.

Then right in the middle of our reminiscing, she said, "I wanted to go back to Virginia and check on things after your father left, but I couldn't leave the three of you. It never seemed to be the right time. . . ."

Her words hung in the air, and I held my breath for fear of what she might say next. Mama sighed: ". . . taking care of three children all alone . . . your father away at war . . . trying to keep the news reports from you girls . . . at least we had our own house . . ." She fell silent.

"Why don't I help you finish weeding the garden?" I said in an effort to change the subject. "Maybe we could drive to Claremore after we get through—go to some of the antique stores and waste the afternoon looking for stuff neither one of us needs. You never know what you might find that you don't need and have to have."

That brought a welcome smile to her face. "Okay, sounds like fun."

We cleaned up the dishes, loaded the dishwasher, and then finished weeding the okra. We were making such good time that we tackled the tomato and green pepper beds as well.

"If we don't get this okra picked soon, it's going to go to seed," Mama observed.

"We don't want that," I said. "Where do you keep your rubber gloves? Maybe we could fry some tonight—and freeze the rest? I bet you have ten, maybe twelve pounds, here."

"Gloves should be in the back of the drawer where I keep my aprons," she said. "Under the hot pads. You'll find a big wooden bowl on the second shelf to the left of the sink, and you'll need a sack as well. There's too much okra here for one bowl. If I don't pick it every other day, it gets away from me, goes to seed, and stops blooming. Be sure you get two gloves, one for each hand, or you'll end up itching for the rest of the day. You remember what picking okra does to your skin."

Everything was exactly where my mother said it would be. The hot pads were stacked neatly with their edges lined up square, and a box of surgical gloves was under the aprons. Skintight, one hundred to a box. Enough to last the summer. Plain old rubber gloves wouldn't do, according to my mother. They wouldn't fit your hands tight the way she thought rubber gloves should when picking okra. Only the aprons seemed unruly, with their uncooperative ties. The bowl, the sacks for the okra, everything else in the kitchen had an assigned spot. It's a shame neatness isn't genetic. My kitchen is always a mess. I can never find anything, and I've never figured out what should go where.

My mother just seems to know where things should go. Every time she visits me, she quietly attacks my kitchen, tucking everything into place with an admonition, "Now, Becky, if you put everything back where I've given it a home, it will always be easy to find next time." And it is easy to find for a while, but then things seem to scatter and get lost again. Neatness eludes me. I snapped the gloves on, made sure I hadn't moved anything from its assigned place, and then headed back out to the garden.

Surveying the rows and rows of okra, I asked, "I'm curious, why do you plant so much of everything? I bet your freezer is already full. Am I right? Nobody could eat this much okra."

Mama made a face at me, ignoring what I'd said.

"When you get through picking the okra, walk it down the street and knock on a few doors. It'll be gone in a snap. I like to give the extra vegetables away. Makes me feel neighborly. Think how many times in the past we wished we had some fried okra. I don't intend to ever run out of it again."

"I don't think you need to worry about running out, Mama. I've never seen so much okra in my life in one place. What's your secret?"

"Horse poop," she said matter-of-factly. "Pat cleans the horse stalls, shovels all the poop outside to dry, and later, after it's cured, as she describes it, she sacks it up and brings it to me. She puts big bows on the sacks for whatever the holiday is. My birthday. Mother's Day. Even Christmas. Best present anyone ever gave me—except for when she cleans the coops. Chicken poop is the best poop. If I have to buy it at the store, they call it manure and charge me ten dollars a bag."

Mama was grinning now, probably thinking about what Daddy would say about that. " 'Manure costs money. Chicken poop doesn't,' or so Pat says."

"Poop or no poop, Mama, you won't use all these green peppers in a million years either."

"Oh, they'll get used. I'll dry some of them. When winter comes, I'll crumble the dried peppers up and put them in meat loaf or on a salad. I won't waste them. Same goes for the tomatoes."

"We all know about your inability to waste anything, Mama. But this year, this once, could we please freeze things in baggies instead of those old grocery bags you drag home from the store and reuse a hundred times."

"Uh-oh, Beebe," she laughed. "Now you've gone to meddlin'."

She had called me Beebe again. It felt good. She had forgiven me for my childhood indiscretion.

"Okay, you win," she said. "This year brand new plastic bags! Now let's finish picking this okra and run away from home."

CHAPTER 46

WE FINISHED WORKING in the garden, sliced and froze the okra, and put some tomatoes in the dehydrator to dry. I walked the excess bags of vegetables down the street to the neighbors, and of course, had to have the *Oh, Becky, I didn't know you were home! It's so good to see you. You look the same as you did when you were a little girl* conversation at every house. Followed by, *Your mother is such a dear, keeping me in tomatoes and okra.*

When you give stuff away in Oklahoma, you have to observe the neighborly protocol of visiting, which is fine unless you're in a hurry, because you absolutely can't act like you're in a hurry. That's considered rude. I was an adult now, but I still followed Mama's do or don't-do list.

After I made my rounds, we drove to Claremore and spent the afternoon going through antique shops, looking. We had spent a thousand yesterdays looking for treasures. On this trip, Mama stumbled onto a piece of pink Waterford Depression glass and tried to justify buying it by commenting on how hard it was to find anymore. I recalled my father telling her once, "You can't find any more of it because you've cornered the market. There isn't any more of it out there because you've already bought it all."

I bought a set of salt-and-pepper-shaker nodders, little china birds that rocked back and forth on a log base. Mama kept a set of bear nodders on her kitchen table. When I showed her the china nodders, she nodded approvingly, "You can't live a proper life without a set of nodders on the table."

On the way home, we stopped for a cup of take-out coffee and bought orange scones at a local bakery for breakfast the next morning, then got on Highway 20. Looking had been fun. Looking had always been fun. The only change was the number of the highway.

We were halfway home from looking when Mama said, "Can I tell you a story?"

"Sure," I said. "It'll make the drive home go faster."

"Okay, well, four months after you were born and Pat was barely eighteen months old, your father was deployed for thirteen months to Japan, in Okinawa. He was flying an airplane the Marines had never operated on a carrier before, intercepting Russian planes to check how fast we could get from ground to contact and interception. Russia didn't like us back then. Actually, they've never liked us."

"You always said he didn't fly airplanes anyway," I reminded her.

She wrinkled her nose at me. "While he was there, I went home to Oklahoma with you two babies to stay with my folks. We didn't have the money for us to stay in California. And to compound the problem, before your dad left to go overseas, your grandmother wrote me and said, 'If you're standing up, sit down. I have something to tell you. I'm pregnant.' What a shock! The doctor said there was no way she could be pregnant, but seven days before you were born, my mom had Lisa. I was twenty-two and a mother myself. My brother was sixteen. And the two of us now had a baby sister!"

"Gee, Mama, your little sister Lisa and I grew up together in Pryor like twins," I said. "Since we were born a week apart, that's what it felt like. I certainly never thought about her being my aunt."

"Neither did Pat! Anyway, there we were. Seven of us. In a very small house, one bathroom and three babies—all in diapers. Cloth diapers. Disposables were a distant future dream. Someone was constantly washing diapers, hanging them outside on the clothesline, or folding and stacking them to be used again on whichever one of you was wet. A continual cycle. Diapers, diapers, diapers.

"Then right before Christmas, my dad—your grandpa—had to have surgery. The operation went well, but the surgeon ordered bed rest for a couple of months. Three squalling babies in the house are the opposite of restful, so I threw the two of you in the car and headed to San Francisco to stay with your father's folks."

"By yourself? Driving by yourself? Did Daddy know you were going to San Francisco? Or did you write him later to tell him what you had already done?" I asked.

"What do you think?"

"Right, dumb question. Easier to ask for forgiveness than to get permission. I guess that's where I inherited that tendency."

"What choice did I have? I couldn't stay where I was. I didn't have enough money to rent a place. And what good would it have done to write and tell your father what I was going to do? He was thousands of miles away on the other side of the globe. Driving to California isn't nearly as dangerous as getting shot off an aircraft carrier. Your father was in an all-weather squadron over there. They operated when no one else could fly—often at night, in storms and other horrible weather. They had the Japanese-Korean perimeter to run every day."

"What did he say when you told him?"

"Who said I told him? He didn't need to know what I had done. He couldn't do anything about it except worry—and he didn't need any more worries. I waited until after we were settled in California to tell him. He would have figured it out eventually when the return address on my letters changed. The day we left Oklahoma, a snowstorm hit. Ice covered the roads, and I lost control of the car before we got out of the county. Did a one-eighty and slid backward down that hill out by the vo-tech school. I caught my breath, said a 'Thank you, God,' turned the car around, and kept driving."

"Good grief, Mama. What were you thinking! Leaving in an ice storm?"

"I know it sounds like a daytime soap opera, but that's what happened. It wasn't so bad once we got on the turnpike headed west."

"Weren't you worried about what might happen on the road?"

"I didn't think about it. Wouldn't have done any good anyway. I did the drive in two days, eight hundred miles a day. The only time we stopped was for gas or to change someone's diaper. Pryor to Texas, New Mexico, Arizona, then on to San Francisco. We arrived at two in the morning."

"Surely you had to stop along the way to eat and feed us?"

"No, I had brought sandwiches, a jug of ice water, Cheetos, potato chips, packages of cheese crackers. This wasn't my first rodeo. I figured a couple of days of junk food wouldn't kill the two of you. I had milk bottles in an ice chest. We had everything we needed and we made it."

"Didn't you consider how dangerous it was for a woman to do back then? Driving through the desert—alone?" I asked her, as all the ways that long-ago trip could have gone bad rushed over me. "Did you consider what might have happened, Mama, if the car had broken down? A woman by herself, no money, two babies. In the middle of nowhere, on some of the most remote highways in the country."

"And my other choices were?" she asked. "Sometimes you have to leave it up to God and get on with it. It wasn't as dangerous as what your father was doing. At night. On a carrier. In storms off the Japanese coast—intercepting Russian migs trying to determine how fast our planes could climb. What choice did I have? I couldn't stay with my parents. I had no money. I had to go somewhere. I had to do something!"

"Knowing you, I don't know why any of this surprises me."

"Anyway, in June, I drove back to Oklahoma with you girls. Five dollars in my pocket and gas money. That's it. The car had no air conditioning, and it was 110 degrees F. when we came through Flagstaff, Arizona. You girls had sweat running down your faces, dripping off your chins. You were miserable. We drove with the windows down, but the heat was so horrible that the air was like a blast furnace."

"It's a miracle you didn't blow a tire," I said. "That kind of heat should have melted them."

"You better believe I was praying. When I got to Flagstaff, I still had nine hundred and eighty-four miles to go. I stopped and used all of my cash—except my gas money—to buy a big round tub. I filled it with ice and put it in the back seat of the car. You and Pat ate ice, played in ice, drank melted ice, and threw ice all over the car. You had a grand time, and the air was so hot and dry that the car dried out as fast as you two got it wet."

"How come I have never heard this story before?" I asked.

"Probably because I didn't want to be a bad influence when you were raising your boys. I hoped you would have better sense than I did and not do such stupid things. But like I said, I didn't have much of a choice. We were lucky. I'll grant you that."

Mama shifted in her seat, slipped off her shoes, then rummaged around in her purse and began to empty its contents—one item at a time, arranging things so they could go back in her purse exactly where they had been before, exactly where, in her mind, they belonged. She found a small nail scissor, cut a loose thread on her sweater, and then started to reload her purse. As I have mentioned before, my mother is extraordinarily organized and neat. Compulsively so.

"So?" I asked her. "What happened after all of that? I assume you made it back to Oklahoma?"

No reply.

My mother's ability to get distracted in the middle of what she's talking about or doing and jump to something else is normal for her, and I knew there was nothing for me to do but wait until she circled back. So I waited.

Finally she said, "That year was overwhelming and unbelievably difficult. Taking care of two babies by myself. Living in someone else's house. Everything that we owned, that was mine, was in military storage at the mercy of circumstance. Biding my time until your father came home. I knew one thing for sure: After thirteen months without your father, we weren't going to have any more babies. Two was plenty. I was done having babies.

"And then, when the thirteen months were finally over, your father had survived that tour on the carrier, and he came home. . . ."

CHAPTER 47

"I HAD PRACTICED WHAT I WAS GOING to say to your father over and over again, and had my little speech memorized. Thirteen months, *thirteen months*, he had been gone—more than a year since we had spoken to or seen each other. Nobody called overseas back then; it was too expensive in 1959, and we had no money. We didn't call. We didn't call because we couldn't pay for it."

"So what did you do?" I asked.

"I wrote letters to him every day all year long, but there was no way he could have known from reading a letter what my life had been like without him because I never wrote him anything sad or bad, just happy or funny—and that I loved him."

"Most women would have complained, Mama. Told their husbands what they were going through with two babies in diapers and no money and living in someone else's house. Gotten a little sympathy."

"That's probably why so many military marriages don't last. There wasn't anything he could have done. Why gripe? His life certainly wasn't perfect either, and he didn't complain when he wrote me." She reached for the sack of scones. "I think I'll try a bite of one of these scones while this coffee is still hot. You want the other half?"

"Sure, why not. If you're nibbling, then so am I. You know, you're a bad influence on me. You nibble all the time and nothing happens. You never gain any weight. I nibble and, well, if I stay here much longer than a week, you'll have to roll me out the door."

Mama shrugged and broke off a piece of scone, wrapped it neatly in a napkin, and handed it to me, saying that if I was going to eat and drive at the same time, I needed to slow down and watch where I was going. And then she picked her story up right where she had left off.

"There was no way I could understand what your father was going through any more than he could grasp what I was dealing with back at home. He was doing one thing; I was doing another. We were living different lives in different worlds."

"How did you manage?" I asked.

"I was so young and full of dreams when he left. Eighteen when we married. Thirteen months later, Pat came along. And then eighteen more months, and you were born. When your dad left for Japan, Pat wasn't yet two, and you were only four months old. Both of you were still babies. Have mercy—I was a baby myself, but life has a way of growing you up. I grew up that year your father was gone. And when he came home, we weren't the same people anymore, your father and I, neither of us."

Before I had a chance to ask what had changed between them, Mama changed the subject again.

"What do you want for supper with that fried okra?" she asked. "How about pinto beans and corn bread? Then tomorrow, you might be able to talk me into frying a chicken. And as long as we're frying, we might as well go all the way. How about mashed potatoes and gravy?"

Her questions barely registered. I was still stuck in the past, thinking about my Marine father returning home to his young wife and two little girls. I pulled myself back to the present and what she had just asked. "I can't keep eating like this, Mama. I'm going to weigh a ton."

"We're having beans tonight—low-cal."

CHAPTER 48

MAMA PUT THE POT OF BEANS on the stove to simmer and went back out to finish weeding the garden. I mixed up a pan of corn bread to go with the brown beans, and after it came out of the oven, I joined her outside. "It's going to be getting dark pretty soon, Mama. Why don't you finish what you're doing and call it a day? Corn bread's hot, if you want a piece—five dry and three wet. Extra sugar."

Mama looked up and nodded. "Flour, cornmeal, sugar, salt, and baking powder—five dry. Milk, eggs, oil—three wet. That's how I learned to make it. Did you know I didn't learn to cook until after I was married?"

"Daddy said he almost starved to death."

"Sounds like something he would say. I couldn't even make Jell-o. First time I tried, I read the directions and thought, 'Why boil the water if you're going to put it in the fridge?' The Jell-o, if you could call that bowl of runny goo Jell-o, sat in the refrigerator a week before I figured out that something about boiling the water must make it set. I had never even used a can opener before that. That's the truth!"

"How in the world did you and Daddy survive?" I asked, unable to suppress a laugh.

"Not very well—I suspect your father made sure he had a big lunch on base every day, but I kept at it, and your dad was a good sport."

"He must have been. I can't imagine you not knowing how to cook. Your mother cooked. Her mother, Gran, cooked. You told me every girl in America had to take homemaking in high school back in the 1950s."

"I took homemaking—four years," Mama said. "I ended up being an excellent seamstress. I made every dress you and Pat ever wore, and not from any old pattern or fabric. Embroidery, tucks, bound button-holes, French seams; organza, cotton, and seersucker. Some of your dresses were so elaborate, I couldn't bear to throw them away when you outgrew them. They're all in a box somewhere up in the attic."

"No! Don't tell me you have more stuff in the attic, Mama!"

"Well, yes, I didn't plan to tell you until you had finished your room, and we cleared out the sewing room. They make quilts at the senior citizen center in town. We can take the fabric there."

"Fabric in the attic? What all's still up there?"

"I was talking about homemaking class," Mama said. "Not the attic—pretend I didn't say that word."

"I'll try, Mama, but I'm afraid that is going to be impossible. I'll probably have nightmares about the attic tonight; I bet my subconscious takes over."

"Well, play Scarlett O'Hara and think about that tomorrow," Mama said. "Anyway, my high school divided our homemaking class into two semesters. The first semester was sewing, which I loved. I did most of my friends' sewing projects for them. To reciprocate, they did my cooking projects the second semester."

"How in the world did you manage to get away with that?" I asked. "I thought teachers were strict back in the old days. Mercy, Mama, I can't picture you doing something that shady."

"Oh, we told the teacher, kind of. I would tell her I was going to give one of my friends a little help, and vice versa. There were so many girls in the class, she couldn't keep up with everything. I don't think she paid much attention to what we told her anyway. The only shady thing I did was to take a friend's sewing project home with me one night—I ripped it all apart and redid it and then returned the finished garment to her the next day. My friend never did learn how to sew. I never did learn how to cook. Honestly, I couldn't see the point in wasting my time on cooking since my mom didn't want me in the kitchen."

"You're *sure* that's the only shady thing you did?"

"Shady? I was trying to help! I redid something for almost every girl in class that first semester. Remember, we had to go through the same thing again the next year, and the next, and the next—sewing came up again every fall and cooking every spring. It wasn't like I didn't do anything when cooking came around. I cleaned up the messes the others made every day. It was an efficient arrangement. Everybody was happy, and we learned to work as a team. I sewed; they cooked. I was happy; they were happy; and the teacher wasn't unhappy."

"Except you *didn't* learn how to cook."

My mother shrugged her shoulders: "True, at least not until after I got married. My grandmother taught me how to make corn bread. That's where I learned about five dry and three wet. My mother never put enough sugar in her corn bread, and your father said it tasted like sawdust. Of course, he never told my mother that, but he did tell Gran that she made the best corn bread in the world! So later, Gran told me how to make mine taste better.

" 'Sweetheart, in this family, we all use the same recipe,' Gran told me, 'but I double the sugar. Everything tastes better with a little bit more sugar. Keeps a man happy.' "

"Well, Mama, I doubled the sugar, so you're going to like this corn bread," I said over my shoulder as I headed back to the house and she returned to pulling weeds. Mama was chuckling as I went inside.

I set the spool-leg table with silver and china, made iced tea, and filled the pink Waterford glasses. Mama came in a few minutes later with mud on her hands, washed up with the milled French soap she always kept by the sink, and began to fry the okra.

"There are some pickled beets in the fridge," she said, "and I found a few scallions in the garden. You get the beets; I'll clean the scallions. Soon as *Wheel of Fortune* is over, we'll eat." We were cleaning up and putting things away when my mother said, "I met him at the Tulsa airport. I went by myself to get him that day, the day he came home.

My first words to him—the speech I had memorized so that I could be sure to get it all said before he could grab me, hug me, pick me up, and kiss me, before he could drag me off—were, 'I can't get pregnant, Ken. I can't. I don't think I could bear it.'

"Your father just grinned at me and said, 'Okay, Babe, now get over here and kiss me like you mean it.' Which I was happy to do, but I wasn't sure he had heard me, so I repeated what I said.

" 'I gotcha,' he said, 'no babies.'

"I guess he understood as much as a Marine who has been gone for thirteen months could understand. He was so glad to see me. I was so glad to see him.

" 'We won't get pregnant,' he promised, and then he picked me up, hugged me, and said, 'But it won't be from lack of trying. What a way to greet a guy! And here I was planning on playing hard to get.'

"His words were greeted by clapping and wolf whistles from the other passengers getting off the plane. He acknowledged their approval with a bow and a big laugh.

" 'This is no laughing matter,' I told him. 'I'm not kidding, Ken. There is no *we* in pregnant. I'm not leaving this airport until you understand how serious I am about this.' I doubt he had any idea how awful—how difficult—another baby would have been for me after the previous year alone with two babies in diapers."

Mama looked up at me with a question on her face. "Am I embarrassing you, Becky?"

"Of course not—we're both grown women," I said. "I don't think the stork brings babies anymore."

"Well, your generation can't imagine life without the pill," she said. "Fifty years ago, we had only a few ways we could even try to prevent pregnancy—most of them far from foolproof, other than outright abstinence, which wasn't an option for either of us at that point. Thirteen months . . .

"Three or four weeks after your father returned home—after we drove to Virginia with the table on top of the car and found a place to live, I got pneumonia and had to be admitted to the hospital. We weren't moved in yet and were still looking for a place closer to base."

"What terrible timing!" I said, shaking my head. "Pneumonia?"

"Pneumonia. Two babies. One car. Me in the hospital—and you and Pat left with a father you barely knew. Pat had accepted him back into the family. You, on the other hand, wouldn't have anything to do with him. You pretended he wasn't there, and if he spoke to you, you would look the other way and ignore him."

"Mama, you don't have to tell me all of this, even though it is interesting. Then again, your stories have always been interesting."

"No, no, it's okay. I want to tell you. Let me finish before I lose my train of thought. Where was I?"

"I wouldn't have anything to do with Daddy after his return."

"Yes, so I had to leave you with someone who might as well have been a stranger to you. I had to be hospitalized. I had no choice and no one else to take care of you and Pat but your father, and he was supposed to be reporting to junior school. He had to miss classes and take leave to watch you girls. He was stressed; I was stressed. More important, I was worried sick about leaving you with him because you refused to let your dad take care of you. Pat filled in as best she could as far as you were concerned—telling your father what you wanted or needed—but my stars, she was only four years old at the time."

Mom shook her head, remembering. "Anyway, they did blood work on me as soon as I was admitted to the hospital. And then . . . and then, the next day, the nurse came in and said, 'Mrs. Jacks, why didn't you tell us you were pregnant?'

" 'Because I'm not!' I told her. 'I am not pregnant. You must be in the wrong room. I have pneumonia. You've got the wrong chart or you've mixed up my tests with someone else's. There is no way I am pregnant. I need antibiotics, not rabbit tests.' The nurse was taken aback by my reaction and apologetic. 'I'm sorry,' she said. 'We'll do the tests again. I don't think there is any way this could be a mistake, but stranger things have happened around here.'

"They did all my tests again. I *was* pregnant. I wanted to die. I even remember thinking maybe I would die of pneumonia, and then thinking maybe that wouldn't be so bad. But I got well—from the pneumonia, not the pregnancy. They kept me a few days, gave me breathing treatments and antibiotics, then sent me home and told me I would be fine. I wasn't fine. I didn't see how I was going to bear it. In the end, I did because I didn't have any other choice: One day at a time. One week at a time. One month at a time.

"And then when I was eight months pregnant, I finally found us a house closer to base. Your father borrowed a pickup and we moved. We piled everything we owned into the middle of the living room at the new house, and I painted the entire inside. I could hardly raise my arms up over my head to paint because all of the stretch in my body had been taken up by my huge stomach, but I got the ceilings painted as well as all the walls, and we moved in. I put sheets on the beds and clothes in the closet and went into labor before I was done unpacking. I didn't get the kitchen boxes opened until I returned from the hospital three days later."

"Mama," I asked. "Do you ever think about that girl—that girl that was you—and wonder how she managed?"

"Sometimes, but then, well, back then it seemed almost normal. You had to deal with whatever life served up." She shook her head and laughed. "Actually, my stay in the hospital was the first time I had gotten any rest in months. You have a baby and the nurses wait on you. They bring you food. They ask if there is anything you need, and, most importantly, they let you *sleep*."

I could tell the experience remained vivid to her and racked my brain for any memory of it, but came up with nothing. "It's funny, Mama, but I don't remember you being pregnant with Amy at all. And I thought you got Scooter from the PX because that's where Daddy said you'd got him."

"My stars! That sounds like something your father would say. He said such outlandish things to you children, I don't know how you turned out normal."

"You think we're normal?"

"No, you three are all exceptional. So I guess your father and I did an acceptable job one way or another."

I reminded her about the tigers, elephants, and rookies. "Daddy never would give me a straight answer about what he was doing."

Mama nodded but didn't respond.

"Did he ever talk to you about it?" I asked.

"No, never—not about dangerous things like his work. I think that was your father's way of coping. All the guys in the squadrons were like that, as I recall. Get a group of aviators together and the stories would be one outlandish tale on top of another with the truth sandwiched somewhere in between. I loved to listen to them brag about their exploits, then hear one of their buddies interrupt with what *actually* had happened. They loved to razz each other. The truth of what their country asked them to do was difficult, but the lies they told about it were funny. Theirs was a language only they spoke. Truth and tall tales. I guess that was how they got through what most couldn't bear.

"I do remember one of the few times that your father didn't make any jokes. I was pregnant with Scooter, and I told your father that maybe the baby would be a boy and wouldn't that be nice? His response was, 'I don't care what it is as long as you and the baby are okay.'

"Later, when Scooter came along, I thought he would be excited the baby was a boy, but that wasn't his reaction at all. When I went into labor, he had to drop me off at the hospital and then run you two girls to the sitter. I had your brother in twenty-six minutes, before your father had a chance to get back. I had the nurse call him at home. She said his first words were, 'Is my wife okay?' His next question, 'Does the baby have all its fingers and toes?' And then he asked to speak to me. He never got around to asking the nurse whether the baby was a boy or a girl.

"The nurse handed me the phone, and when I said we had a boy, his response was, 'Are you sure?' I told the doctor what your father had asked, and the doctor promptly held Scooter upside down by his feet, jiggled him up and down, and said, 'He's got all the equipment.'

" 'Well, isn't that something!' your father replied."

The room fell quiet.

"Where was I?" Mama asked.

"You were telling me about when Scooter was born, but it's okay—it's getting late. I have maybe another hour to finish my room—why don't you tell me the rest of the story tomorrow? I want to hear how it ends," I said.

"That's a good idea," she said. "I forgot where I was anyway."

"What do you want to tackle tomorrow as far as the house?"

"Let's start on the sewing room."

"Sounds like a plan. Don't set the alarm. We'll start on it right after orange scones and coffee."

"Brush your teeth and say your prayers," she said.

"Good night, Mama. See you in the morning. I'm going to finish those few things in my—I mean, the guest bedroom, and I'm off to bed."

"Becky, it is not a guest room. It's *your* room; I still think of it as your room. When I vacuum in there, I always expect to find a mess under the bed because of all those times I told you to pick up. You always just shoved everything under the bed."

"That's because I never could figure out where it all went."

"Even though I know that's true, I find it utterly unbelievable. I used to think you were just stubborn, which you are, but I also suspected the hospital might have switched babies on me when you were born." She smiled. "But your eyes are brown like mine. And your smile is mine. You're mine, all right."

It was my turn to smile. I did have her smile and her brown eyes. Her neatness gene? Well, that hadn't skipped a generation, but it had skipped me. I headed upstairs to finish the odds and ends left to do in my room, then hauled another bag of trash to the garage. I brushed my teeth, put on my pajamas, and said my prayers with every intention of calling Pat. As I crawled into bed, however, I saw my journal on the nightstand next to my angel lamp where I had left it that morning. I picked it up and turned a page or two.

> Crabs don't grow in Oklahoma. Just snails and tadpoles and turtles. Oklahoma doesn't have an ocean, just a creek. I hope I have time to teach my daddy how to roller-skate before he . . .

I fell asleep without ever turning the light off, and dreamed of Saline Creek all night long. We were in the car, driving somewhere—on top of the water, with tadpoles swimming along beside us, snails sitting on the front like hood ornaments, and turtles on roller-skates following along behind us. Overhead, airplanes dropped bombs; the flashes caused by the explosions lit our way.

Where were we going? I had no idea.

I woke up the next morning exhausted and realized I had forgotten to call Pat.

CHAPTER 49

A STEADY RAIN GREETED me in the morning. No wind, which was unusual in Oklahoma this time of year. Gale-force winds tended to come with the rain. "You can always tell an Oklahoma woman," my father once said. "She holds her head facing into the wind so it won't mess up her hair."

I pulled on a T-shirt and jeans, tied my hair back in a ponytail, padded barefoot to the kitchen, and made myself a cup of Earl Grey tea. I could hear Mama, already rummaging around in the sewing room. I brewed her a cup of Darjeeling and went to see what progress she was making. When I found her in the laundry room, I wasn't sure whether to laugh or scream. She was on top of the clothes dryer holding a couple of boxes, with a confused look on her face.

"What are you doing up there?" I said. "Why didn't you wait until I got up so I could help you? Mama, you're lucky you didn't fall and break your neck."

"Good thing you came along then," Mama said, feigning outrage. She looked around from her perch atop the dryer. "I've always loved these ten-foot ceilings with the extra storage of the higher cabinets, but I do seem to have gotten myself in a pickle here."

"You are definitely in a pickle," I said. "Come on—hand me down those boxes. Take a seat on the dryer, and I'll get a chair so you can hop down. How in the world did you get up there? I do hope you appreciate that I'm not yelling at you for getting stuck."

"Is that tea for me?"

"Yes, Darjeeling."

"Good, thank you. I could use a cup of tea right about now." Mama handed me the boxes, crawled off the dryer onto the chair, brushed herself off, and then took the fabric boxes from me. "It's dusty up there."

"Please tell me you aren't getting up there again—to dust?"

"Okay."

"Okay what?"

"Okay, I'm not getting up there again to dust. Let's take our tea into the kitchen and reheat the rest of those orange scones in the microwave."

"Only if you promise that after tea, the two of us can tackle the sewing room. Together. Okay? And if there is any climbing to do, I'll be the one to do it."

"You think I can't do it by myself?" Mama said in a huff. "I would have figured out how to get down off the dryer eventually. I woke up at four and saw no need to waste time waiting for you to get up. Anyway, I didn't want to disturb you. You need your sleep."

Something in her voice made me wonder. "Mama," I asked. "How long had you been standing up there on the dryer?"

Silence.

"I could point out that you could have cleaned this fabric out anytime in the last ten, twenty years, but you didn't. Say uncle, Mama. You know you don't want to do it by yourself."

Mom took a sip of her tea and said, "You're right. I don't want to do it by myself or I would already have it done. And you're also right that it would take me forever to do it by myself. So *uncle*! I'm glad you're here. I'm glad you're helping me. And I'll be good!"

"Only until I'm not looking or you see something else that you want done right that second," I muttered under my breath, loud enough so she could hear. "Can we agree that if there is any more climbing to do, I'll be the one to do it? You promised not to dust up there, but I don't know what else you might find to do that requires climbing up on top of something. It's kind of like trying to figure out what to tell Scooter not to do."

Again, silence.

I followed her into the kitchen. I wasn't sure she had heard me. She was putting the scones in the microwave. I took that to mean the conversation was over. I didn't know if I had won or not. Probably not. The microwave dinged.

"Your scone is done," she said. "Truce?"

"Well, okay, since you said *uncle*. Truce."

Mama grinned at me as she got two small plates and removed the scones from the microwave. "How many calories do you think are in one of these?" she asked. "The orange icing alone must have at least . . ."

"Please don't ruin it!" I said. "Let's think about calories tomorrow."

We nibbled on scones, sipped tea, and discussed what to do with the contents of her various boxes—what to keep and how to dispose of the lace, rickrack, elastic, snaps, buttons, pins, needles, and other sewing notions that she would likely never use again.

"I want to keep a few of each one in case I have to mend something," she said. "The rest of it can go."

"Do you intend to mend anything ever again, Mama?"

"Well, no. But if the mood happened to strike me, and if I had a few sewing notions left, I could. You can throw out all the zippers and the bias tape. And I won't need all that fringe and lace. Leave me the pins and needles and some buttons and snaps."

With that settled, we finished our tea and scones, loaded the dishes into the dishwasher, and wiped off the table.

"Do you want to tackle the rest of the sewing room now?" Mama asked. "Or we could wait and do it later."

"We might as well get on it. It's not going to go away," I said. "I'm ready if you are. Let's see how much we can get finished before noon."

We were sorting fabric and sewing notions when she surprised me by up and breaking the silence, saying, "It was sudden . . . so sudden. Your father was rocking Amy while we watched TV, but it was bedtime for you girls. I took the two of you to get into your pajamas. That's the last memory I have of Amy . . . your father rocking her, smiling at her, telling her how pretty she was.

"What in the world was wrong with me? Why had I been so adamant about not having another baby? Amy was so sweet. You couldn't help but adore her. When the nurse gave her to me to hold for the first time, I looked at this precious little girl and told her, 'Why Amy, I didn't know it was you inside my tummy or I wouldn't have been so miserable.' You know how it is; you look at your child and it is immediate adoration, immediate love. Whatever worries you had before evaporate when the baby arrives."

Mama looked down at a piece of soft pink flannel she was holding, and I wondered if there was a story behind it as well.

"That night I put you girls to bed, and when I rejoined your father, I suggested he try putting her in her bassinet. He was reluctant. 'Ken, you've been rocking her for an hour, and she's still fussy. Maybe she's tired of being held. It's almost time to feed her anyway. I'll go get a bottle.'

"Your father put her in her basket, then went to read a bedtime story to you girls. I fixed Amy's bottle—it took three, maybe four minutes. Five at the most. When I returned, she was lying in her bassinet. And suddenly. Suddenly. How do you describe something so unthinkable? I picked her up, but the beautiful little baby girl we adored was gone. She had slipped out the door of our lives without a sound. Quietly, peacefully."

Amy's departure from this world might have been peaceful, yet as I watched my mother twist the scrap of soft pink flannel tighter and tighter I knew what had come next had not been.

"Afterwards, it wasn't about her," Mama said. "It was about how she changed your father and me. One moment she was here, and the next moment . . . she wasn't. That's everything. Everything except your father giving her mouth-to-mouth resuscitation, trying to breathe for her. I tried to get you and Pat into the car; I was in such a panic that I dropped the car keys and had to get on my hands and knees to find them. It seemed like an eternity before I did, though it was probably only a few seconds. Time had stopped.

"Your father breathed for Amy while I drove like a crazy person, with a couple of patrolmen behind us trying to stop me for speeding until they pulled alongside and saw your father. Then we had an escort blocking all the lights, clearing traffic ahead of us the rest of the way to the hospital.

"We didn't have 9-1-1 back then; we didn't even have a telephone book. We had only moved in the week before. They must have radioed ahead, because the gate was wide open at the base, and hospital attendants were standing outside waiting for us. One of them took Amy from your father's arms before I could even stop the car and took over artificial respiration."

I watched as Mama turned her attention back to the boxes of fabric. She opened one, pulling out a piece of baby blue wool.

"See this gorgeous wool?" she said. "I bought four yards off a truck for pennies way back when we lived in California. I still love it. Those are angora nubs, the white part. This fabric is so pretty, and I was always afraid that I would choose the wrong pattern and mess it up, so I kept thinking and thinking about how best to use it. All these years, and I never got around to doing anything with it. And here it has been. Sitting in a box on a shelf. Never used."

She sighed as she set the blue fabric aside. "There was this fellow who would drive into Escondido in his beat-up truck, drop the tailgate, and sell fabric out of the truck bed for cash. Every woman on base knew where he would pull up and park. That blue wool is still the softest I have ever touched. Just remembering the day that I bought it still makes me smile."

"Mama, this entire house is full of things that make you smile. That's why you still have it all, but if you remember, that's why I'm here. I'm trying to help you figure out what to do with all of it."

"I'm keeping this," Mama said.

"And how many other pieces?"

"Not many. I promise."

CHAPTER 50

MY MOTHER WAS TRUE to her word. The stacks of fabric destined to leave the house continued to grow. Pretty soon the boxes were all filled, and I was taping them shut. "You'll have to call your friend Gail in Saint Louis. Tell her we have some fabric for those women who make quilts for charity. Her group and the senior center are the only ones I know who might use it. No one else I know around here quilts anymore. For that matter, nobody knows how to sew anymore. Sewing is a lost art—girls don't take homemaking in high school; they take bull riding, truck driving, engineering, or some other such thing."

"I'm an engineer."

"See, what did I say?"

"As I recall, Mama, you were the one who insisted I take all that math and science. In eighth grade, when I wanted to enroll in engineering drawing and the school wouldn't let girls take the class, you're the one who marched down to the junior high to speak to the principal. Before I knew what had happened, I was enrolled—along with two other girls."

"Well, for pity sakes, what else was I to do? It was the 1960s. A revolution was going on. Figured I might as well participate. Just because no female had ever enrolled in an engineering class at that school before didn't make it right. I was a little disappointed, actually. They gave in so quickly—only took an hour or two of reasoning with them."

"Them? Them who?" I asked.

"Them who made the rules. By the time we were through discussing it, the principal had called in the superintendent, and he had called in the instructor of the class. Three men. And me. They wasted quite a bit of time trying to explain why they didn't enroll girls in that class—their main reason being that having girls around was too distracting for the boys. So distracting, they feared, the boys wouldn't be able to concentrate on engineering drawing. And they pompously added that girls aren't going to become engineers anyway."

"Are you kidding? Is that the reason they gave? Or are you making this all up to entertain me, as Daddy used to say?"

"Distracting the boys—yes, that's what they said. I was polite. I didn't argue with them; I just didn't agree with what they were telling me. And I didn't budge. Two hours later, when they realized I wasn't going to change my mind and I wasn't going away, they changed theirs. Reluctantly. I was prepared to hold a sit-in if words didn't work. And, yes, me and Rosa Parks changed the world. Never would have occurred to me that I could protest like that if Rosa hadn't done it first. And before you correct me, I know, I should have said Rosa Parks and I."

I had to laugh—she looked so proud of herself, correcting her own English. "Mercy, Mama, I can't picture you doing that. On the other hand, not losing your temper or telling them how silly their rule was, I *can* picture that—since you are usually polite. The idea of you sitting there refusing to move until the rule got changed, well, I would like to have seen that."

My mother grinned. "What were they going to do? Call security? Call the sheriff? They had to know that if they refused, my first call would be to my friend Hack down at the local paper, and he would have made sure that the inequity made the front page of the next day's newspaper. Every reporter in America was looking for such stories at the time. Mine would have prompted every mother in town to march to the school with picket signs to join me.

"Rosa Parks—that quiet dignified woman who refused to go to the back of the bus—turned the world upside down simply by saying, 'No.' Hard for your generation to imagine how many doors were closed to women forty years ago. Rosa's moment was a victory for the civil rights movement, but I've always contended that she did a lot for all women that day. She empowered us. Men ran the world back then. I'm not saying men were bad people. That was just how the world was and had always been. Girls weren't engineers. Or doctors. Or lawyers. Or Marines."

Her story of doing something on my behalf all those years ago made me smile—telling it had left her with a warm glow of satisfaction.

"I fought my own little war after that victory at your school. A year later, I enrolled in a calculus class at the local junior college—only woman in the class. Five white boys, thirty-five Iranians, and me. That was back when our government liked the Shah of Iran, and young Iranians came to the United States by the droves to go to college. I passed the class first try, along with a couple of the boys. None of the Iranians passed, at least not the first time they took it. That might have had something to do with their not speaking English—you had to admire them for even trying. I tried not to be offended that the consensus of educators at the time was that women weren't mathematical. Maybe I had a small part in refuting the conventional wisdom—if only in my neck of the woods."

"Good grief, Mama! How do I not know any of this? I suppose I should say thank you. I made an A in engineering drawing, and so did the two girls who enrolled with me. Only one boy did that well. I do remember the teacher seemed surprised—he'd been pretty patronizing to us girls the whole semester. The next year, half of the engineering class was girls."

"You girls started a mini revolution," Mama said.

"No! You did!" I said. "I was only thirteen. I didn't know you could do something that the principal said you couldn't do."

"Well, now you do." She turned her attention back to the fabric.

When the last box had been filled and sealed, I carried them out to my car, knowing that Mama would never pay postage to ship them to Saint Louis when there was a chance someone in the family would be going there eventually. We were making progress. Most of the boxes were out of Mama's house, and that was a good thing—fewer boxes of stuff inside, fewer memories from the past to bump into.

The next day, we puttered around the house doing a whole lot of nothing. Mama sorted summer clothes and filled a bag with items for the Indian mission in Salina, Kansas. I went through old magazines and filled another box to go to the nursing home. Little by little, we discarded and organized, as we'd done a million times while in the military.

Moving was a dominant memory of my childhood.

For my mother, moving was a skill set.

Midmorning, we took a sweet tea break, and as I made a list of to-dos for later, Mama thumbed through a copy of *Southern Living* magazine. She seemed restless. So I wasn't surprised when she put the magazine aside. She picked up a shoe and slipped it on, took it back off, and then began to fiddle with the shoestring. I had noticed her glancing over at me as if she was about to say something. When she finally spoke, she picked up her story where she had left off—as if it had been minutes and not twenty-four hours ago.

"We went into the emergency room. Your father and I. We sat there and waited. Finally, a doctor came in with a chaplain and said, 'I'm so sorry.' And then he asked, 'Are you Protestant, Catholic, or Jewish?' For the life of me, I couldn't figure out what difference it should make—I was still trying to figure out why he had said he was sorry. What else was there for him to say? Amy was gone. We buried her at Arlington, across the street from the Tomb of the Unknown Soldier. Almost fifty years ago—though it seems like yesterday. In my mind forever, she will always be nine days old, rocking in your father's arms."

"How did you bear it, Mama? How did you bear the loss?"

"I just did, as well as a twenty-three-year-old girl could. When you're that young, you don't think about such things happening. You're in shock. It almost killed your father. Marines live every day with the possibility that they might be, or one of their friends might be, lost—but his child? How could he even imagine such a thing?

"Your dad kept saying, 'I thought it would be me. I was prepared for it to be me. I've spent the last fifteen years protecting our country, and I was ready to make that sacrifice. Why wasn't it me? Why couldn't I save her?' He could not accept that there was nothing more he could have done. The doctor at the hospital assured him repeatedly, 'You did everything that you could possibly do, Major. Sometimes there are no answers for why these things happen. You did everything exactly the right way. I couldn't have done any better. This was not your fault.'

"But for your father, trying to revive her had been so personal, pressing her small chest over and over again, trying to make her heart beat again. The fact that he couldn't revive her haunted him. Afterward, we went months without discussing what had happened—trying, I suppose, to avoid causing each other more pain or distress. Your father was probably asking himself the same questions I was agonizing over, questions that always began with the words 'What if I—' but no, we never talked about it. We just went on. I locked it all away. There didn't seem to be any point in talking about it. It was done. Over."

My mother's matter-of-fact recollection faltered. Before I could ask if she was okay, she said, "Losing her was only part of the pain. After she was gone, I couldn't seem to bear life without her. I was eaten up with guilt. I couldn't help but think God was saying to me, 'You didn't want the baby I sent to you, the one that I had planned to give you, so I took her back.' "

"No!" I said before I could stop myself. "You know God isn't like that. If anyone knows that, Mama, you do."

"Yes, yes, I know that's true. I was trying to make sense of why she was gone. It was too late to explain to God that I had changed my mind, that I wanted her—too late to ask for mercy, to beg for forgiveness for not trusting him while I was pregnant. That part almost killed me. It felt as if a dark curtain had fallen over me, and I didn't know how to find my way out into the world again."

"But you did," I said. "Despite everything, you did. You were a good mother; you were always there for us."

"No," she said. "Not really. I was going through the motions that next year. It's hard to imagine how alone a wife can be in the military unless you've been one. Friends and family are everything at times like that, and I didn't have either nearby. Pat started kindergarten; your dad went back to work. My family was in Oklahoma. You and I were left to ourselves. I had to try and figure it out all by myself. I was lost. Totally, utterly lost."

"What about the folks from your church? Didn't some of them come and help?"

"The church? Oh, no—they barely knew us. I'm sure, under other circumstances, they would have tried to help, but your father and I moved so often, nobody got to know us. We always joined the nearest Baptist church and explained our situation to the minister: 'We are Bible teachers. If you call our last church and check us out, it will save time, and we'll be able to serve while we are here—before we have to move again. Otherwise, we'll be gone to the next duty station before you get to know us or have time to decide where you want to use us.' They usually put us to work teaching a Sunday school class and skipped the getting-to-know you part."

Once again, I found myself wondering how she had never told me any of this before. I doubted she had told anyone else either. Knowing my mother, I guess I shouldn't have been surprised. When you're a military wife, you never stop moving. The Marines believe in forward motion—no matter what happens, that you have to keep moving forward. Grief? Regret? The past? Not so much.

"I don't hold anything against anybody at the church," Mama said. "They didn't know. That's just the way it was. The way it had always been for us. I remember right after we were married, I played the piano for a Baptist church in Warrington, near Pensacola. We were only there three weeks before they had me playing the piano for the choir. Within a week, they had checked me out and received approval. They didn't have a pianist and I could play. It wasn't the normal way to find a place to serve in a church, but telling someone what I could do up front saved a lot of time as the years went on.

"In Virginia, after Amy was born, we were attending the church at Triangle, a little town near the base at Quantico. I was working with the youth, twelve- and thirteen-year-olds. I didn't know any of the adults. We weren't permanent. They knew it. We knew it. So no, we didn't have anyone from the church reach out to us.

"We were military. Enough said."

"What about folks from the base?" I asked. "Surely there must have been someone at Quantico. Someone like Dr. Phil and Jeanette? If the Golfeders had been living nearby, I know they would have helped."

"Quantico, Virginia," Mama said, "was a different arrangement than South Carolina. Your father was no longer in a squadron; he was in junior school. If he had been in a squadron, you're right, it would have been different. The people in a squadron are a lot like family. When you were born, your father was in a squadron at El Toro, and I got a taste of that. Twenty-five aviators and almost two hundred support personnel, and those pilots were like brothers. The wives took care of each other. If something went wrong in one of the families, everyone pitched in and helped. But junior school at Quantico, well, that was a random group of unconnected people from different Marine specialties—men that had made field grade or major and had been tapped to go to junior school. Your father might have had some casual friends. I had no friends at all."

"Do you have any friends left from Daddy's active duty days?" I asked. "Anyone besides Jeanette?"

Mama seemed to think for a moment. "No, not many. As a matter of fact, I made my first real friend right after we were married, after we left Pensacola and moved to California to Camp Pendleton. Your father was the air officer for the Seventh Regiment; those Marines were all ground pounders. No pilots. "I was nineteen years old, married thirteen months, and half a continent away from my family. I didn't know a single soul. I was pregnant with Pat. And I'd never been around a baby before. I didn't have a clue what to do with her. Ignorant doesn't begin to describe it. There was only one book on the subject at that time, and it was written by a man, Dr. Spock! A man! Can you believe it? What did a man know about having a baby? Or being a new mother? No other books, no self-help videos, no nothing—videos hadn't been invented yet anyway. What I needed was *Babies for Dummies*."

"I can't imagine," I said. And I meant it—her world in the 1950s might as well have been on Mars.

"Anyway," she said, "after we transferred there, I met Mary Lib. She befriended me. Lib explained that everyone in the neighborhood was 'ground,' and that our husbands were 'aviation,' which was why no one on our street was very friendly. I was so new to the military, I had no clue about the difference between the air wing and the battalions and regiments. Lib explained that after a year with ground pounders, our fellas would move to a base where they would be back in squadrons, and we would probably never see any of these people ever again. She said some of the ground pounders' wives were a little resentful too. They thought our husbands were rich—because they got flight pay. Truth was, we were as poor as they were because aviators had to use all that allowance to pay for hazardous duty flight insurance.

"After ten years as a military wife, Lib's grasp of Marine life was helpful. More importantly, she showed me what to do with a baby. How to hold it, burp it, feed it. How to fix a bottle. For a young girl who couldn't even cook, caring for a baby was daunting. We became friends because she made the decision to be my friend. I don't know what I would have done without her.

"Five years later, Lib showed up at our house the day after we had buried Amy. I didn't know that her husband had been transferred to Quantico and assigned to junior school with your father until she walked in our front door. They had only been on base a week. She walked unannounced into my bedroom where I was curled up in bed and said, 'I'd have been here sooner, but I just heard. Get up. You aren't sick and this won't do. Hand me that sheet.' I did what she said, and she started to rip the sheet into strips.

" 'Stand up. Take off your pajama top. I'm going to bind your breasts so they don't fill up with any more milk. You aren't going to lie there and suffer because your boobs ache. I know they hurt, but if we don't do something quick, they're going to get worse.'

"I did what she told me to do. What a relief it was to have someone take charge of me. When she was done, she said, 'Get your clothes on. We're going shopping. You aren't dead yet, and neither are your two little girls. You're going to be all right someday. Maybe not anytime soon but someday. Right now, you need a little push so you can get on with the rest of your life, because it isn't over yet.'

"And so I started to live the rest of my life."

I had listened to my mother's story without asking many questions. She had told this part mostly in one fell swoop, as if a dam had broken somewhere inside, and everything of consequence had spilled out.

"Lib was my friend. She was my friend, my *only* friend, when I needed one. She's gone now. It might be silly, but I like to think she's up in heaven rocking Amy. We wrote each other for years, but when she left her husband—he was an unfaithful jerk—she moved to Florida, and my letters all came back, no forwarding address. I'm sure she didn't know where we were either. She took back her maiden name, and it was years before I found her again."

"When Lib came to the house that day, did you tell Daddy?"

"No."

"Did you tell him about any of it?"

"No."

"Why not?" I asked.

"What good would that have done? Your father was in the middle of school. He couldn't quit to hold my hand. I couldn't stop taking care of you girls to hold his. We were still adjusting to his return home and the recent move. We had to keep on keeping on. That was our way of life. You did what you had to do. If you didn't, life unraveled—I've seen it happen before and since. Some families never recover."

"That was when you and I started looking for treasures," I said. "Daddy was in school and Pat was in kindergarten. Do you remember? I had you all to myself back for a spell. I had so much fun. Those days are among my happiest childhood memories."

"I'm glad you have happy memories from that time. I guess I must have done something right then. It didn't seem so to me at the time. I was on autopilot. I just kept getting up, fixing breakfast, washing clothes, making lunch, reading to you girls, going to the grocery store, cooking supper, putting you to bed. Smiling when I was supposed to smile. Listening when I was supposed to listen. Like I said, one foot in front of the other—always moving forward."

"You would say, 'Beebe, let's run away from home today.' "

"I remember," she said. "You would get so excited that we were going somewhere together, just us two."

"You and I were living parallel lives but different realities," I told her. "Yours was sad and lonely. Mine was perfect—happy and full of you. I remember everything about that time. The places we went, the things we looked at, the stuff we bought. When I wander through this house and see something we found that year, I get a warm and fuzzy feeling. I really do."

Mom smiled at me and said, "Eventually, you and Pat rubbed off on me, I suppose. Eventually, the two of you mended my brokenness, and one day I found that I could be thankful again. I had two perfect little girls.

"It's just that, well, once I had three."

As I listened to her, I couldn't help thinking how you can live under your parents' roof and never know the stories behind the smiles or their scars. The scars you see and the ones you don't.

You think you know them, and then something shifts, and you realize you don't know spit.

CHAPTER 51

HEAVEN WAS ENDING. We were leaving Beaufort. We were moving. Moving was hard on Pat and me and Mama. Daddy and Scooter were oblivious. Daddy because he was never there for the organizing part. And Scooter because, well, he was Scooter. Scooter was oblivious to everything—all the time.

Mama had a million to-dos on her list that had to be finished before we could make the move from South Carolina to Oklahoma. The worst to-do was getting the house ready for inspection. With everything else going on—between the twin disasters of finding clothes for all of us to wear and Daddy's changing of command ceremony—there was no time to think about what the inspectors were doing at our house.

We had been cleaning for weeks to prepare for them. Pat and I had been assigned to scrub off all the marks on the walls below three feet, most of it Scooter's artwork. Mama had tackled the walls above three feet herself, along with the stove, refrigerator, and bathrooms, all of which had to be spotless. Military spotless.

"I don't know why we have to do this," I told her, " 'cause the military's going to paint anyway. Every time anyone on our street moves out, they paint. Every single time. What's the point?"

"Because," Mama said. "Not 'cause."

"Why *because?*"

"Because I said so."

In the end, maybe the clean walls helped after all, because the house passed inspection. As we piled into the car to leave, we took one last look at our home of the last three years. We never heard if the inspectors returned to paint it or not. The clothes on our backs and the things the women on our street had rounded up for us were all the five of us had. That and a cat Pat had adopted earlier that week and had begged to bring along.

"She won't be any trouble, Daddy," Pat said. "I will take care of her and hold her all the way."

"No! We not taking a cat with us in the car," he said. "You don't even have a leash. Or a collar. Or a name. How will you let her out to do her business without a leash?"

"We can stop and get a leash and a litter box," Pat begged. "I'll put the leash on her and keep the box on the floor. Please, Daddy? Please?"

"No way there's going to be a litter box in this car," he said.

"We came to South Carolina with a dog in the car, and now he's gone to heaven, and the cat is a lot smaller than he was," Pat pleaded. "We can stop and get a leash and collar. I have my allowance!"

The cat purred as we left South Carolina behind. Daddy had never been able to say no to his oldest daughter. As for me, I clambered to my knees in the back seat of the car and looked out the rear window to catch one last glimpse of the home we were leaving. Something somewhere inside me ached. I thought of all the other places we had lived in my short life, as well as the places my mother and father had lived before that. They never went back. So I knew I was probably never going to see Beaufort again.

We drove for miles with no one speaking. The silence roared. In the end, we didn't stop and get a collar or a leash or a litter box for the cat because Scooter fell asleep, and Mama was worried that stopping would wake him up. She looked exhausted and thankful for the little peace and quiet that came with a slumbering Scooter.

So Daddy drove on—headed west in his dress blues with Mama in her red dress and Pat, Scott, and me in our borrowed clothes. He drove until it was dark trying to find a place to stay for the night. We stopped at every motel for miles, but a highway patrol convention was going on in the area. Every motel was full. "There's a base a few miles ahead," my father told Mama. "I think it's Army, but maybe it will have a hostess house or somewhere we can stay."

We ended up in a tiny room with two single beds in an old barracks set on cinder blocks. Daddy hung up his dress blues and Mama her red dress, and in our underwear, all five of us crawled into bed. Mama, Pat, and I shared one twin bed, Mama in one direction, me and Pat in the other with the cat between us. Daddy and Scooter shared the other bed. We were all so tired, the sleep arrangements didn't matter. Sleep was instant.

The cat started to meow at about six o'clock the next morning. I poked Pat awake to deal with the cat before she woke anyone else up.

"What are you going to do?" I whispered to my sister. "You have to let her out, but if you do, she'll probably run away."

"No, she won't," Pat whispered back. "She will come to me when she is through."

"She hardly knows you," I said. "She might not come, and then what will you do?"

"Just be quiet, and don't wake Mama or Daddy. Come with me. You get on one side of the barracks; I'll get on the other. She'll come to one of us when she's done."

But the cat didn't. We both coaxed, "Here, kitty, kitty."

The cat didn't budge. And at seven, Mama came looking for us. "What are you two doing running around outside in your underwear? Get in here and get dressed right now. You should both be ashamed of yourselves, acting like tater-shed children."

That's when Pat started to cry. I couldn't believe it. My stoic sister crying! At first, I thought Pat had been upset by Mama's tater-shed comment. Then I realized her tears weren't because Mama was upset with us.

No, Pat was worried about what our father was going to say. "The cat is under the barracks and won't come out," Pat sobbed, "and Daddy is going to be upset with me because I let her out without a leash. But she had to go, and I thought she would come to me because she loves me. But she didn't. So maybe she doesn't love me, and I don't know what to do. Mama, please bring my clothes out here because I can't leave her. She might run away!" Pat was bawling by then.

"Don't fret, Sweetheart," Mama said. "I'll get your father up; he'll know what to do."

"I'll go get Pat's clothes, Mama," I offered, "If you'll take my place on this side of the barracks—be ready to grab the kitty if she comes out this way."

"That won't be necessary," Mama said. "I'll get Pat's clothes. I'll get your clothes too while I'm at it. I can't believe you two girls are running around in your underwear."

"Daddy's going to leave the cat here," Pat wailed, as she hiccuped between sobs. "I know he will! He said bringing her was a bad idea. He'll say she'll just have to find a home somewhere on base after we leave. He didn't want me to bring her in the first place, and now . . . and now . . . and now she won't come out!"

"Let me take care of your father," my mother said.

Mama gave Pat a quick hug and went back inside where, as usual, she must have worked her magic on our father, because a few minutes later, Daddy came outside in full dress uniform. Without a word, he got on his hands and knees, and crawled underneath the muddy barracks toward the cat.

"Here, kitty, kitty," he called. And for some reason known only to the Almighty himself, the kitten came to him.

"Oh, Daddy, thank you!" Pat said.

"Her name is Kitty," my father pronounced. "That's her name now."

"Kitty," my sister replied. "Yes, that's what I think it is too."

Daddy heaved himself to his feet, still holding Kitty, just as an Army platoon marched by, counting cadence in perfect unison. It had rained in the night, and Daddy's uniform was covered with mud. Each of the soldiers saluted him and not a single soldier broke rank or showed even a trace of a smile. Daddy returned their salute as if everything was as it should be, and it was not unusual for a Marine lieutenant colonel in full dress uniform to be covered in mud from tip to top and holding a cat—a kitty cat.

After they had passed, Daddy heaved a sigh and handed Kitty over to Pat. "Good grief, I'm glad we're only passing through. I hope I never have to explain this to anyone," he said as he unsuccessfully tried to brush the mud off his uniform. "Thankfully, I won't be needing this dress uniform where I'm going. Everybody get inside, get dressed, and get in the car. Pat, hold on to that cat. First store we see, we're stopping to get a leash and a collar for Kitty and a change of clothes for me."

Within minutes, we were all in the car and officially on our way to Oklahoma. Beaufort was behind us.

What lay ahead? Who could possibly know?

Such is the normal state of affairs for a military family.

CHAPTER 52

UPON OUR ARRIVAL IN PRYOR, the first thing I noticed was that nobody in town seemed to know anything about the U.S. Marine Corps save for a few veterans of World War II. However, everyone did seem to know who we were. That's because everyone knew our grandparents. In the neighborhood where we bought our house, the kids had known each other their entire life and had never moved—some of them had never traveled beyond the state border, some not past the city limits.

They stared at us like we were aliens.

"Where didja come from?" one boy asked.

"South Carolina."

"How come?"

"Our dad has a new job."

"He git fired?"

"No, he got orders. Right now, he's on leave."

"Somebody giving him orders. Making him leave?"

"No, he wasn't ordered. He wasn't pushed around. He was transferred. He got orders. He's on leave."

"Right. Ordered 'round. Had ta leave."

I shook my head and went into the house—no point trying to explain an elephant to a blind man.

Church wasn't much different than the playground except the questions were a little more polite and the folks asking them old enough to be my grandma or grandpa. "Your daddy's in the Army now—isn't he."

A statement, not a question. "No, Ma'am, he's a Marine."

"Martha," the lady called to a friend. "Come over here and say hello to little Becky and Patty. They're Margie Swan's granddaughters. Their daddy flies airplanes in the Army." Like I said, hopeless.

"Things will get better," my grandmother told me afterward. "Give them a little time. Almost everyone in Pryor works an eight-to-five job in the industrial park like their parents did. They don't understand moving around. Or the military. Or fighter pilots."

The people of Pryor may not have known much about military people, but the place did have its attractions. One was Saline Creek. And as he had promised, Daddy found time to take us there. We spent a wonderful day catching frogs, crawdads, minnows, and snails—there weren't any hermit crabs like in Beaufort, but the Oklahoma critters were interesting. By afternoon's end, we were sunburned—no surprise, and our bodies were covered in freshwater leeches—a slimy surprise. The long-tailed, slimy blood-sucking worms felt weird on our skin but did no real harm. We just picked them off one by one, wrapped ourselves in towels, and trudged to the car, where we stripped off our bathing suits and donned our clothes behind it, hoping no one drove by. The ice-cold water had left us shivering and with quivering blue lips for the ride home. But no one complained.

On Saturdays, we went roller-skating. Our father had never been home for such a long, wonderful stretch of time. Then four weeks later, he was gone. One day he was there; the next day, he wasn't. No mention was ever made about where he had gone.

The night before he left, I heard him wandering about the house, making soft shuffling noises as he gathered up his gear and tried not to wake anyone. His efforts were unnecessary. We were all awake, even Scooter—awake waiting for our daddy to come and kiss us goodnight as he always did before he had to leave.

"Goodbye, Punkin," he said to me when he kissed my forehead. "You be good and help your mother."

I heard my sister in the hallway. Daddy always told her goodbye first, but instead of her staying in bed afterward, she was up and softly sobbing. "Daddy," she said. "Please don't go. This time, why don't you tell the government you can't go?"

My father picked her up and cradled her head on his shoulder. "You have to be strong for Becky and Sam," he told her. "Your mother is going to be lonesome. She needs you. You're the oldest. You have good sense, and you make up for all the crazy things that happen in this family when I'm away."

"The cat," she whispered. "I'm so sorry about your uniform. I should have listened to you and left the cat behind."

"Don't you worry about my uniform. You needed Kitty. I understand. Where I'm going, I won't wear dress blues anyway. I probably won't ever need that uniform again."

"I love you, Daddy," my sister whispered.

"I know you do. And I love you too. You are the only sensible child I have. Try to keep Becky and Sam out of trouble. But if you can't, that's okay. It's probably an impossible task with those two. I'm going to miss you. I'm sorry, but you'll have to get your mother to brush your hair while I'm gone."

By then, everyone was out of bed, trailing my father to the door.

"I'll write," he said. "I'll number the envelopes in reverse so you'll know how many days are left until I come home. On every letter, the number will get smaller."

My mother touched his hand, and he traced a soft line from her cheek to her chin. He hugged me next, patted my brother on the head, and said, "Sam, you try to be a good boy."

And then Daddy was out the door.

One week later, the first letter came. Numbered three hundred and eighty-six.

Thirteen months.

A lifetime.

CHAPTER 53

Pryor, Oklahoma
2010

THE NEXT MORNING, Mama and I looked around and pondered what to tackle next in the house. She picked up a picture in an antique frame from the mantel. "This was taken before we left Beaufort," she said. "Before your father left that last time. I guess he wanted to be sure we had at least one family picture of all of us from a happy time in our lives. Just in case."

She set the picture back down and said, "I told him I was going to take you kids and move to Olathe, Kansas, to live in base housing while he was gone."

" 'No,' he told me. 'This is not up for grabs. I'm not going to worry about you and my children while I'm overseas. I'm going to have more than enough to worry about on the other side of the world. You aren't going to go to Olathe. You need to be in Oklahoma where your people are, where your mom and dad can pick up the slack if you get sick or something happens and you need some help. We're going to buy a house there. You need to be somewhere permanent just in case . . .'

" 'But some of the other pilots' wives are moving there, to Olathe,' I told him. 'I would have support up there, and the housing would be free as well.'

" 'No. Period. We're not discussing this. I'm not going to spend every day of the next year wondering whether you and the kids are okay. If something should happen to me, well, I have to know that you have a home, that you and our children are settled with your people, your mom and dad—so, no. You aren't going to Olathe.'

"I remember being shocked—it was the first time he'd ever said no to me. But he was so adamant that I didn't argue. Your dad was always easygoing, so when he refused to even discuss the matter, I took a deep breath and said, 'Okay. We'll go to Oklahoma.' "

I chuckled. "He must have been in shock when you agreed."

"Well, I'm usually agreeable when I'm facing a brick wall."

"I'd say that's up for grabs, Mama."

CHAPTER 54

I STARTED SCHOOL the day after my father left to go overseas. I was the new girl. I didn't know the name of a single person in my class, which would not have been a problem except for the fact that everyone else in the class had known each other since they were babies. My name was the only new name they had to learn. Me, I had to learn a couple of dozen.

All heads turned when I entered the classroom. The teacher introduced me to the class: "Children, this is Becky Jacks. Her family moved to town this summer. Her father is in the Army, and he flies airplanes."

"He's a Marine," I quickly corrected.

"What did you say, Miss Becky?" the teacher said.

"He's a Marine!" I said with conviction. "He's not in the Army. He's not in the Navy or in the Air Force. He's not in the Coast Guard." I felt better already. "He's not in anything; he is something: He's a Marine."

The classroom went dead quiet. I had contradicted the teacher on the first day of school. Everyone in the room, including me, held their breath to see what punishment the teacher would dole out to the new girl. I had been in this kind of situation before, and I was prepared to take my punishment. I had defended my father and it felt great. He was a Marine. That was a fact. While I waited to hear what the teacher was going to say or do, I couldn't help wondering if anyone else had ever been sent to the principal's office in the first ten minutes of a new school year. At a new school. No one was more surprised than me when the teacher simply said, "Okay, Sugar," and in the same breath, told us to get out our math books.

How lucky can you get? School was going to be a breeze. A teacher who asks questions but doesn't listen to your answers. What was there not to like? Unfortunately, when the teacher set about reviewing where the class had left off the previous year, second grade quickly began to look no better than first. I already knew my multiplication tables. I had been hoping for some long division, but it became clear that wasn't going to happen.

I took a Nancy Drew book out of my backpack, propped it behind my math book, and read for the rest of the hour. I had my sister to thank for that. "Take a book with you to read every time you go to school, or you will go crazy," Pat had told me before we left for our first day of school. "Prop it behind your textbook and no one will be the wiser."

Her advice kept boredom at bay for the rest of the day. When I got home from school that day, the house was empty. Nobody anywhere. A neighbor from across the street called out, "Are you Becky?"

"Yes, Ma'am, I am Becky. Do you know where my mother is?"

"Well, Sugar." Everybody calls you "Sugar" in Oklahoma. "Your brother hit a swarm of bees with a broomstick. Your mother had to take him to the emergency room. Last I heard, they had given him a shot and were pulling stingers out of his hair. Your mother's with him."

"His hair?" I repeated.

"Well, not his *hair*, his head. They've already pulled the stingers out of his face and hands. Luckily, the rest of him was covered with clothes. Your mama called to say he's going to live, but it was touch and go for a while. He was stung more than a hundred times. She said he blew up like a balloon from the swelling. Bless his heart. She asked me to tell you and your sister what happened. Said she'll be home as soon as she can."

"Thank you," I said, giving her a little wave as I headed up the driveway. My response, or rather my lack of response, had probably left the neighbor wondering what part of the story she had failed to deliver with enough drama. Obviously, she didn't know my brother and his ability to find a new way to scare us all to death on a regular basis.

I let myself into the house and headed for the kitchen. After pouring myself a bowl of Cocoa Puffs, I plopped down on the couch to watch *The Gumby Show*. During the commercial breaks, I pondered my brother's fate. If my brother was a cat with nine lives, he'd be dead already—and he's not even old enough to go to school yet. I waited for Pat to get home while I worried about Scooter. My father's admonition for him to be a good boy was pretty well shot.

Later that evening, Mama brought Scooter home. Pat took one look at him and announced, "He doesn't look too good." Then she told our little brother, "You look like a puffer fish." When Scooter began to cry, however, Pat immediately went into wounded-creature-rescue mode. She chopped up some ice, wrapped the ice in a tea towel, and dabbed Scooter's poor, pitiful face with the cool cloth.

"This will make you feel better," she told him.

Like I've said before, my sister knows what to do with hurt things. I don't. My only contribution that night was to ask Scooter if he would like to watch television with me. "Come watch *Gumby*," I said. "I'm sorry you hurt." What else was there to say? My brother was a certified idgit, as Pat would have said under any other circumstance. Who in his right mind swats a swarm of bees?

Not long after school began, Pat turned nine, and everyone in her class was invited to a party at our house, despite the local practice of asking only five or six friends.

Fifteen kids showed up, ate a ton of ice cream and cake, poked holes in a piñata, and went on a treasure hunt. The next day, everyone at school was talking about Pat's party, and anybody who hadn't come realized they had missed something special. Overnight, we became an accepted part of local society. Mama had worked her magic—and endeared us to all the parents in town—by inviting *everyone* in Pat's class.

"Heard 'bout your sister's party," one of the boys in my class told me the next day.

"Whatudja' hear?" I was doing my best to talk Okie English at school while juggling proper English at home. It wasn't easy. I was far from fluent in either of them.

"Everything—they said you had a treasure hunt! My brother missed it. Kickin' hisself in the butt, he is. Missed th' fun."

"I'll be eight in April. We'll have another one. You can come." I didn't tell him that he shouldn't say *butt*. No need to make an enemy.

"Be there. Yep. You gonna have another piñata thingamajig?"

"Sure. My mom will make one. She made my sister's, and I helped her fill it up with candy."

"Cool," he said.

I gave him a little wave and stepped away before I could mess things up. I couldn't believe it! One of my classmates wanted to come to my birthday party! Maybe school this year wasn't going to be so bad after all. Maybe, I would make a friend. Maybe, when I made a friend, the friendship would last. Maybe, they wouldn't move.

Maybe, we wouldn't move either.

Maybe.

CHAPTER 55

WINTER CAME, BRINGING bitter winds and ice storms that only an Oklahoma native could believe. At times, ice hung so thick and heavy that it split big trees like kindling and littered the ground with dead branches. Trees fell on houses and cars. Roads were blocked with fallen tree limbs. School was canceled—as well as church. Ice had made the roads so slick they were impassable by car and so deadly on foot that the nearest hospital filled up with folks, young and old, with broken hips, legs, and arms.

On the winter days when school was open, we walked to class with our eyelashes frozen by the time we arrived. My mother didn't believe freezing temperatures or ice were a reason for her children to stay indoors. So we bundled up, and out we went until she called us in for supper. If the weather got too bad, we were relegated to the garage. I longed for the balmy breezes of South Carolina.

At five o'clock every evening, our TV was turned off. Mama told us that after 5:00 p.m., there was nothing on TV fit to watch. Soon enough, I figured out what she was doing. She was making sure we missed the evening news. She had refused to subscribe to the local newspaper when the paperboy came around to sign her up. So unlike my evenings with Dr. Phil and the Philadelphia newspaper, I had no way to know what was going on in the rest of the world, especially the particular part of the world our mother didn't want us to hear about.

Almost every day, a letter from my father—or several—came in the mail. And every night at seven, before getting ready for bed, my mother would write one to him in return. She always asked each of us kids to add something at the bottom. "Where are you?" I wrote in my best longhand. "Please let me know so I can find it on the map at school."

"We miss you, Daddy," my sister added. "Thank you for writing to us. We check the mailbox every day hoping for a letter. We love you. I'm doing my best to watch over my brother and sister, but Scooter is impossible. Guess what! Kitty has kittens—six of them."

Mama always made sure to include Scooter as well—asking him what he wanted to say to Daddy and adding his remarks to the letter in Scooter's own unique English. "Whaz'up, dude? I'ze all stung. The nurse shaved all my hair off."

And then, one day, the letters from Daddy stopped.

None of us said anything about it, but as day after day went by with no letter, the fear I held inside grew. At school, talk sometimes turned to a war going on in a place they called Vietnam.

"Them POWs is all pilots," one of the more self-appointed informed members of my class told us. "Some of 'em, those POWs, been in them there prisons since that there war began."

"Where?" someone in the class asked.

"What prisons?" someone else said.

"What war?" another asked.

"You know," the boy said. "The war where they're fighting them gooks. Gooks wait till them flyboys 'jects, and then they nab 'em and put 'em in the Hanoi Hilton my uncle says. My uncle was in the big war, World War II. He knows about that there stuff. He told me all 'bout them POWs and . . ."

I interrupted him. "You aren't supposed to say *gooks*. That's not a nice word." I didn't know anything about a hotel or what a POW was, but I wasn't about to let on and risk looking like an idgit. And I knew better than to call anyone names. I had asked my mother about the word *gook* after seeing it in Dr. Phil's Philadelphia newspaper. My question had caused such a ruckus with Mama that I had no intention of ever asking her about the word again. But who could I ask? My teacher? My preacher? I decided to ignore what my schoolmate had said. Sometimes it's better than looking stupid.

At home, Mama continued to check the mailbox every day, and every single day the result was the same. The mailbox was empty. It had been eight days. Pat and I had been counting.

One afternoon when I got home from school, I decided it was time to get Mama to answer some of my questions. I tested the water with an easy one, since questions weren't my mother's favorite thing.

"Mama," I said, "what's a POW?"

Without missing a beat, she said, "It's a pesky old woman." And before I could ask anything else, she added, "Which I think I'm going to be if you don't quit asking questions all the time."

"You're only in your twenties, Mama. You don't get to be old 'til you're thirty. Grandma said so."

"That's good—means I have two more years; although, I feel as if I'm a million years old already."

"Mama?"

"What?"

"The letter, the next letter—when is it coming? Why has Daddy stopped writing to us?"

Sometimes, it seemed like every crisis in my life had been over a letter. And, yes, I might have crossed the line mentioning that the letters from Daddy had stopped, but I had crossed the line so many times already in my short life that once more couldn't possibly matter all that much. I didn't mention Hanoi.

I could look that up on the map at school.

"I'm praying one will come soon," she whispered.

Soon couldn't come soon enough, I thought.

CHAPTER 56

TWENTY-THREE DAYS PASSED before the letters began to come again. Letters 221 all the way down to 198 arrived the same day. We read them in order all at once, huddled around Mama. Ecstatic that there were letters again. Thrilled that the 200 mark had been broken.

> *I know you must be concerned, but I have been in country with no regular mail run. I've been working on putting down a Marston-matting runway in the jungle, and just today someone was able to land on it, and we were able to get the pilot to fly our letters out. We have been so busy. We laid a runway like this one back when we lived in South Carolina. You remember, that was the time I couldn't come to the hospital when Becky was so sick. That's what I was doing, figuring out how to lay matting in a jungle. But this is an entirely different project here, knowing how to do it and getting it done are two different things, and it's kept us hopping.*

My dad never complained in his letters. He rarely told us much of what was going on either. But in one of the letters that came that day, I could almost feel his misery.

> *I am living in a tent. It has rained for seventy-two days in a row, and my fingernail clippers have rusted in my pocket. The tent is wet, the floor is wet, my bed is wet. Everything is completely soaked with no hope of it ever drying out. I've been volunteering for extra missions just so I can break through the clouds and see the sun again. I dream of home. Of my family. And wonder if this year will never end. If I ever again set foot on American soil, I promise to God that I'll never leave home again.*

In another, Daddy told us something he probably thought was funny, but the effect was to generate concern. Mama hummed that passage, leaving Pat and me a bit confused and ultimately thinking the worst thing our father was dealing with was too much rain and a soggy bed.

> *I got hit on my last mission. I had delivered my load and knocked out a loudspeaker that was harassing our ground troops. I was flying low and pulling up out of the run when a fifty-millimeter round went right through the cockpit. I had just leaned forward to pull back on the stick, or it would have cleaned the wax out of both my ears. I know the same God that watches over me takes care of you too. . . .*

Mama quit humming. "Now, where was I?" she said.

> *Sam, stay away from bees. Everyone worries about me, but it seems to me that you are the one we need to worry about.*
> *Pat, I hear you are reading Nancy Drew books in school instead of paying attention to your teacher. As long*

*as you make As, I say power to you, but if you bring home
a B, the books have to go. I know you are bored. Maybe
if you put your Nancy Drew behind your textbook, it
wouldn't irritate the teacher so much. Not that I'm
advocating rebellion, just trying to help you keep the peace
at school.*

I guess Daddy didn't know Pat had not only figured out that hide-a-book-in-a-book technique but had taught me to do the same thing.

*Becky, thank you for all you do to help Pat keep your
brother from driving your mother crazy. It has to be a full-time job, and I am sure at times it seems like a mighty
impossible one.*

Mom started to hum again as she read, and this time, she did so under her breath in a whisper so soft I only caught a few words.

*Sweetheart, you know where my heart is. I long for
the day when I can . . . This nightmare is almost over—
more than halfway done. I have flown seventy-six mis-sions. Twenty-four to go and I can come home. Piece of
cake. One good thing happened. I got another squadron,
VMA-311.*

Our preacher says there are two kinds of sins: The ordinary kind that we do without thinking much about and the premeditated sins that we know are wrong, we think about how wrong they are, and then we go ahead and do them anyway. After dinner that evening, I excused myself early from the table—I didn't even stick around for dessert. And then I did a sin. A sin I had been thinking about ever since Mama put the letters away. I went to her room and got the letters out of the chest where she kept them. What can I say? She didn't say *not* to do that. And then I read them. All of them. I couldn't say what I had hoped to find in the letters, but I did learn one thing: Mama hummed for a reason.

Mama was humming the parts of Daddy's letters that she didn't want us kids to hear. And after reading those parts of the letters myself, I thought I knew why: Those were the scary parts and the parts about how much Daddy missed her.

I slipped the bundles of letters back where I had found them and shut the lid on the chest. I must be getting close to the accountable age, because I felt horrible afterward. I had done something I shouldn't have done. I had read something I shouldn't have read. And worse yet, I knew doing it was wrong before I did it, even though no one had told me not to do it.

I wasn't sure I wanted to be accountable.

CHAPTER 57

OKLAHOMA BEGAN TO MELT in March; spring was nearly upon us. Crocuses popped up and daffodils nodded along the driveways. The yellow flowers grew in patches on vacant lots where someone had planted them in a long forgotten yard. The second week in March, pink tinges appeared on the redbud trees, and by the third week, the redbuds were in full bloom. Every yard in the county had a redbud tree bursting pink and pretty, and just when you thought it couldn't get any better, the dogwoods bloomed—some white, some pink, along with peonies and astilbe and lilies. Spring in Oklahoma almost made up for the icy winter. Almost.

Then it was April and I was eight years old. Everyone in my class came to my birthday party except for two boys who had the mumps and three girls who had chicken pox. Everything was the same as it had been at my sister's party except that a few moms this time asked if they could help. One of them even brought homemade ice cream! I think those moms wanted to see if it was true that everyone in my class was invited. They were.

Although my birthday party was fun, I missed the neighborhood parties back in Beaufort when everyone on the block gathered in our backyard in the evenings. Entire families. Adults bringing potato salad and pies and cakes with their ice-cream freezers packed and ready to churn, while we kids caught fireflies and waited for the ice cream to set. I was lonesome for the whine of the jet planes overhead and for the spooky oak forest we used to play in at night, scaring ourselves silly as the owls hooted and the crickets chirruped their songs. I was lonesome for the Spanish moss trailing from the trees, blowing gently in the sea breeze, and something else that I couldn't quite explain.

"I miss Beaufort, Mama," I told her as we cleaned up after my party. "I don't want to grow up."

Mama set down a stack of plates and turned toward me. "Well, I've heard it said that when you know you don't want to grow up that you are finally grown up," she said to me. "Maybe you are older than eight, and we just forgot to count a year or two back when we were living like gypsies."

"I'm eight, Mama. You know how old I am."

Mama shook her head and picked up the plates. As she headed for the kitchen, she said, "Well, you have to go forward, Sugar. You sure can't go back to Beaufort. We live in Oklahoma now. Looking back can make you sad or it can make you glad—glad for all the wonderful memories no one can ever take away from you. You get to choose. I have a little secret for you: The only way to be happy is to be happy now. 'In everything give thanks; for this is the will of God in Christ Jesus concerning you.' That's what Paul says in the Bible. Thankfulness gives you a happy heart. You might start a thankful journal—maybe that would help. For right now, could you bring in the rest of the glasses from outside? I need to get these into the dishwasher."

I called after her, "I don't want to start a thankful journal. I'm not thankful, and I don't want to know what the Bible says. I just want my daddy to come home. It's been so long since I've seen him that I can't remember what he looks like anymore. What if he doesn't remember me?"

With that fear confessed, I choked up, ran to my room, and shut the door. All my feelings and fears were out of the bag. I took so many deep breaths trying not to cry that I hyperventilated and had to put a paper bag over my head. But I didn't call for help. I just breathed slowly into the sack. I knew about hyperventilating from my science class, so maybe I had learned something useful in school after all this year. That should have cheered me up—that the school year hadn't been a total waste. But it didn't.

I didn't want to be happy right now.

All I wanted was for us to be a family again.

I began to cry, softly so no one would hear me.

CHAPTER 58

SUMMER IN OKLAHOMA WAS A brand-new experience. Temperatures soared to ninety degrees F. and then over a hundred. The only time you could play outside was early in the morning before the sun came up or after the sun went down or if it was raining. Unless the rain came with a lightning storm. Or a tornado. Storm cellars—the locals called them fraidy holes—were furnished with chairs and plenty of snacks because we used them so often. After a while, the wild swings in the weather seemed normal to me. Even the tornadoes. The sirens would blow, and everyone would start running, yelling, and counting heads to make sure they had all their kids as they raced for the cellars. It wasn't unusual to get into the cellar and realize that someone was missing. Then the real excitement began, especially when the warning came at night.

One night, the wind was so strong I could barely stand.

"Where's Scooter?" my mother yelled over the howling wind.

"I'll go back and find him!" Pat shouted.

"No, I will!" Mama cried.

"No, Mama, sit down!" Pat insisted in a loud voice I had never heard her use before. "I couldn't stand it if something happened to you.

I've already lost one parent to God knows where, and I'm not going to take a chance on losing another one." To my astonishment, Mama did what Pat said. Until that moment, I don't think my mother had ever thought about our father being gone from my sister's point of view.

Pat soon returned with my dead-to-the-world brother sound asleep and thrown over her shoulder. Drool ran down his chin. "He was in his bed—out like a light. He's still out," my sister said as she handed Scooter over to my mother.

"Thank you," Mama said. "Now let's get this cellar door down and shut tight before the real wind hits."

In Oklahoma, there is wind. And there is *real wind*. And then there is hundred-mile-an-hour-or-more tornadic wind. Even the plain old Oklahoma everyday wind can reach sixty to seventy miles an hour and more than twice what it would take to bowl over a girl Pat's size carrying a sleeping boy. No wonder everyone in Oklahoma talks about the weather and everyone—young and old alike—has an opinion about it. Oklahomans shared a strange pride in the audacity of their state's weather. "If you don't like the weather," the locals would say with a chuckle, "wait a minute and it'll change."

Which was true. Storm season, as it was called, began in late March and ran usually into mid-June. Or sometimes longer. The weather is fickle in Oklahoma. Weather news trumped all other news. TV stations ran their weather report at the beginning of the hour, which meant Mama could let us turn the television on in the evenings for it without fear that other news would intrude. I guess she thought we didn't know why she let us keep the TV on for only a few minutes in the evenings. But Pat and I knew why she didn't want us to watch the news. We knew.

By now, I had told Pat what I had read in the letters from our father. I think we would have known even if I hadn't read Daddy's letters. Kids know stuff. No words required.

Between the thunder storms and the brutal heat, we stayed pretty miserable all summer. No matter how hot it was, however, my brother and the other boys in the neighborhood could be found playing baseball in the vacant lot across the street. That is, until they broke a neighbor's window and were banned to the schoolyard. Scooter would come home covered in dust, with streaks running down his face and body where the sweat had parted the dirt, grinning from ear to ear. Occasionally blood would be mixed with the sweat and dirt, which he never seemed to notice.

"Lemme tell ya how great I is," he would say. "I hit a 'omer."

"Get in the tub. You stink and you're filthy," my mother would say. "Let me have those clothes. They're so dirty; I'll have to wash them twice. Three of us girls, and all I do is wash boy clothes. You rip up everything I get you, Scooter. You look like a tater-shed kid. I don't think you're happy unless you're bleeding and your clothes are torn and dirty."

And then, just when you thought the weather couldn't get any worse, the late August furnace turned up a notch, burning everything in its path, turning the grass so yellow and brittle that it crackled when you walked on it.

We stayed camped inside where the air conditioner ran full force, reading books and playing Parcheesi or gin rummy. Monopoly was still our favorite game. Everyone wanted to land on Boardwalk—until someone bought it, and then we never wanted to land there again. I sometimes wondered if Andy had anyone to play Monopoly with now.

I realized I missed him. He had been such a pest.

But a nice, familiar pest.

CHAPTER 59

MAMA HAD DECIDED THAT summer vacation was the perfect time for us to become cultured, so she enrolled Pat and me in piano lessons and then sentenced us to practice an hour every day. At first, I didn't think being cultured was going to take, but after a while, the scales and chords began to resonate somewhere inside me, and playing the piano became fun—a change probably abetted by the fact that there wasn't much of anything else to keep you occupied in the triple-digit heat of August in Pryor.

My father had been gone almost a year. It might seem strange, but we never *ever* talked about where he was—and Mama continued to censor the news. She didn't know that Pat and I knew all about the war. We knew where Hanoi was. Not talking about Vietnam didn't make the war stop or the worry go away. The worry should have abated as the numbers at the top of my father's letters got smaller, but it didn't. Days and days lay ahead. They seemed longer than the days behind us.

My mother's blackout of the news had been a clever ploy, but there were other TV sets in other houses where we went to play. We watched. We knew. And her silence about what America was up to on the other side of the world became a shared silence as we three pretended not to know. Lest our worlds be shattered by words said to each other that wouldn't help and couldn't be taken back.

Vietnam. The word alone was chilling. My father was a Marine, a fighter pilot. My classmate had been right: Almost every POW in this stupid war was a Navy or Marine pilot. If they ejected and safely cleared the plane, sometimes they were lucky and got picked up by a friendly helicopter. Often they didn't. Sometimes the pilot got picked up by the North Vietnamese and taken to the Hanoi Hilton. If a pilot didn't eject or if he didn't get picked up by his buddies or if he didn't go to the Hilton, then that meant—what? My eight-year-old heart had frozen because deep down I knew the answer to that question already. He didn't make it. He didn't come home. Counting the days was agony.

When school started, there were only a couple of new kids. Everyone else was the same as the previous year. None of the teachers had moved, and neither had any of my classmates. It was strange for me. Our teacher from the year before said hello and called each of us by name as we passed by her classroom. Weird. Everyone knew each other's name. That was how it was in Pryor. Everybody knew everybody else. And now I knew them too. It all seemed so, so . . . *permanent.* My older sister and little brother had been my only permanent friends before this. I wasn't exactly sure what the rules were for making a permanent friend, much less being one. Whatever the rules were, I wasn't ready for that just yet. I didn't know if I ever would be. I hadn't ever experienced permanent before.

August slipped into September, which faded into October and then November. Dad had left in November the year before. He had been gone a year now. He had one more month to do. We had one more month to wait. An eternity. We held our breath as the numbers on the letters from my father slipped into the teens. Nineteen, eighteen, and then a letter came that said that this was the last letter he would be writing. The letter was numbered fourteen. Mama didn't even bother to hum through any of it.

I'm processing out. I have five more hops, and then, probably in four weeks, God willing, I'm checking out and

*coming home. This war is almost over for me. I wish it
was over for everyone.*

God willing, I will see you soon.

*But I've been thinking. When I get back, I have to
serve three more months in California at El Toro before I
can retire. My resignation has been approved, and if—
no, when—I get back, I don't want the girls to have to be
uprooted from school again, so why don't we plan on all of
you staying there while I do those three months in California? I'll fly back and forth to Tulsa on the weekends, and
you can pick me up. I'll take two weeks leave to be there
with all of you in Oklahoma—before I go to El Toro.
Surely, after all this time, we can make it three more
months. Then I retire. Piece of cake. We can do it.*

Who could imagine thinking about California, school, or what was
best for Pat or me at such a time? All we could think of was whether or
not Daddy was going to survive this last month overseas before he could
come home to us. Five more hops. You would think this last month
would be easy, knowing it was almost over, but getting through those
last weeks was horrible—worse than the twelve months that had gone
before. When you're getting shot at every day, the possibility that you
could end up in the Hanoi Hilton always exists.

Or worse.

Worse things could happen than the Hanoi Hilton.

I tried not to think about that until I said my prayers at night.

*Please God, let them miss him. Don't let them hit his
plane again. Just let them miss him four more weeks. Five
more hops.*

I no longer started my prayers with, *Now, God, you better listen to me*
. . . I had given up the attitude when my daddy left.

Now all of my prayers started, *Please, God. . . .*

CHAPTER 60

ONCE AGAIN, THE LETTERS stopped. Was my daddy processing out? He had said, *a month*. That was three more weeks away. What could have happened to stop the letters? Fear kept me, for once, from asking Mama the question I wanted to ask. The following Monday, my sister and I were late getting out the door for school when Mama realized Scooter was missing. "Where's your brother? Hold on, girls—let me find him so he can walk to school with you two."

Hunting for Scooter had become a regular morning delay since our little brother had started kindergarten. Getting him there—on time—was a daily ordeal. Once we found him, he nearly always had to be cleaned up and his clothes changed because he would already be too dirty to be presentable for school.

On this particular morning, Mama found my brother before he could ruin his clothes. She opened the front door and we grabbed our backpacks, dragging Scooter behind us.

"I don't wanna go to school," Scooter protested, pulling his shoes and socks off, hopping on one foot, and stuffing his socks in a pocket. "I went yesterday and it *wudden* any fun. We *diden* get to go outside but two times!"

Pat and I were still on the front porch, trying to get his shoes and socks back on him when a dark sedan pulled into the driveway. A tall officer in full uniform with a short beard got out and began walking toward us.

"No," my mother said under her breath. "Oh, dear God, no."

She grabbed Scooter and began to push all three of us back into the house. Once inside, she shut the door behind us and locked it.

"Do not open that door!" she ordered.

"Mama," Pat said, "that won't make the man go away. You're going to have to talk to him."

"No, no—no, I don't."

I had seen Mama do this once before, and so I knew she wasn't going to be letting the man in. She wasn't going to talk to him either.

Pat pulled the drapes back on the front picture window a bit and peered out. I peeked out too. We watched the officer slowly climb the steps of the front porch. And then, something about the walk. Familiar but different somehow. Tired, older. I could hardly breathe.

Pat threw open the door. "Daddy?" she whispered.

"Isn't anybody going to give me a hug?" the man said.

Pat and I tumbled out the front door and fell on him with kisses and hugs. He held us. We held him. We didn't let him go until Scooter pushed between us.

"Are you my daddy?" he asked.

"I am. Are you my Sam?" my father replied.

"Yup. I's Sam."

Mama had held back until then. She stepped forward now and touched my father's hand as if she wanted to be sure he was real.

"How? We didn't expect you. Not for two more weeks. I thought you were the chaplain. I thought you were . . ."

"I know, I know." My father reached for my mother and wrapped his arms around her. "I'm sorry. They let me go. I did my five hops, and the general told me to get on the next plane and go home. I haven't changed clothes, taken a bath, or shaved in I can't remember how long. I left Vietnam with what I have on. I would have called ahead if I could."

As the shock of seeing our father began to wear off, the joy of having him home suddenly called our daily routine into question. "Mama, do we have to go to school?" Pat asked. "Daddy, can we skip school? Please, Daddy, please!"

Before Mama could respond, Daddy said, "Of course, we're all taking the day off!"

He gave Mama a big squeeze. The conversation swirling around me seemed trivial. I stood there silently taking it all in until my father looked my way.

"Hello, Punkin," he said. "You're all grown up."

"You didn't eject? You didn't go to the Hilton?" I said.

"No, I tried a couple of times, but the Hilton was full." And then he whispered almost to himself, "It was full . . . full of my friends."

A sadness appeared in his eyes. I didn't dare ask how many of his friends were still prisoners in Hanoi. I touched his short beard, laid my head against his chest, and whispered to him, "Mama doesn't like beards. You better shave it off."

"That's the first thing I'm going to do," he said and reached for my mother's hand. "And the second . . ."

Mama took his hand, raised it to her cheek, and laid her face softly in his palm.

"Shave," she said.

CHAPTER 61

MY FATHER LEFT FOR CALIFORNIA two weeks later. "Three more months. We can do it standing on our heads," he assured us. We weren't so sure. Saying goodbye to him was terrible. I didn't understand how he could think leaving us behind in Oklahoma was a good thing. What was he thinking? We went to school the day after he left and tried to take up life where we had left off, but that proved impossible.

"School is stupid," I said to my sister as we walked home that afternoon. "Stupid! We know everything we're supposed to know already."

"I could have skipped the fifth grade completely," Pat agreed, "and you sure don't need what they are teaching you in the third."

"True, but you're a certified genius. You shouldn't have to go to school at all," I said.

"That was one stupid test," my sister said. "Doesn't mean anything. Anyway, don't you go around telling anyone about that. Kids don't like it when you're smart, and I have a hard enough time making friends without *smart* hanging over me."

Truth be told, nothing was actually wrong with school. Pat and I were the problem. Moving had forced us to learn things that most kids don't usually learn when you live in one place all your life. We had been forced by circumstances to learn how to cope, and reading had exposed us to even more of the world—the good and the bad—as had military life. When we walked in the front door of our house after school, the tantalizing aroma of chicken frying greeted us. Mama fried chicken only on Sundays, so something was up. Daddy hadn't been gone twenty-four hours, and she was frying chicken.

"What's going on?" Pat asked.

"We're going to have a family meeting after supper," Mama replied. "You two go finish your homework. Then practice piano until I get dinner on the table."

A family meeting? We had never had a meeting before of any kind. Never. Ever.

"Why are we having a family meeting?" I asked.

"You'll have to wait and see," my mother replied.

Wait and see? I stomped off to my room. I hated to wait.

Scooter came dragging into my bedroom before I could cool off.

"What in the world did you do to get so dirty?" I asked him. "You look like a pig, a pig that's been rolling around in the mud. Get in the tub—wash that mud off and put on some clean clothes because something's up. Mama's called a family meeting, and you have to be presentable. You look like a tater-shed kid."

"Whaz up?" Scooter asked.

"I don't know. Neither does Pat. Just hurry! Mama's almost done frying a chicken, and it's not Sunday. Whatever it's about; it's serious!"

"Yum!" Scooter hadn't gotten past chicken being on the menu. Off he went down the hall, shedding his clothes as he sang, "Yum, yum, yum, and a bottle of Pepsi." Being a Baptist, Mama wouldn't let him say *bottle of rum*. The last thing I saw was his bare butt as he went through the bathroom door. I didn't say *butt* out loud, so I didn't sin. I just happen to know one when I see one.

Dinner was as good as if it had been a Sunday. We ate the whole chicken. All the mashed potatoes, little green peas, and gravy were also finished off. And then Mama sat up straight and announced, "I would like to call this meeting to order. Is everyone present?"

"Yes." "Yes." "And yup," we answered.

Pat and I elbowed our brother and hissed in his ear, "You don't say yup in our family!"

"I *meaned* to say, 'Yes um, Mama,' " Scooter said.

"*Meant to say,*" she replied.

"Yup," he said, "that's what I *meaned* to say."

Pat rolled her eyes and silently mouthed to me, "Hopeless."

Before Mama could get distracted again by Scooter's English or lack thereof, I spoke up.

"Mama, I'll help Scooter with his English later. Could we get on with the meeting, if that's okay with you?"

"That would be fine, Becky, thank you," she replied. "Now, where was I? Oh yes, I've called this meeting because you three children have been through a lot over the past year with your father gone. He has no idea what it's been like for the three of you, but I know it has been very difficult. And since he left yesterday, I've been thinking about that, and so I think we should vote."

"Vote? Vote on what?" Pat asked.

"I think we should take a vote on whether you want to finish school here in Oklahoma or go to California and be with your daddy and go to school out there for the next three months. I'm going to let you three choose what you think would be best."

"California?" Pat said.

"We get a choice?" I asked. "We get to vote on it?"

We had never before been given such a choice. I was pretty sure Mama was joking. And just as I was about to ask her if she was kidding, she said, "All in favor of going to California, raise your right hand."

Four hands shot up. All of ours, including Mama's.

"Then it's decided," my mother declared as she lowered her hand. "Dump everything out of your backpacks, your school books, papers— all of it—you won't need any of that in California. Pack yourselves a change of clothes, along with your Sunday clothes and shoes and any- thing else you want. I'll get the black skillet and whatever else we can't live without and start packing the car. Remember—the basics. Only the basics! There isn't much room in the car."

Pat and I were speechless, but Mama was already working her way down her packing to-do list.

"I'm turning off the air conditioner and locking the doors. I'll call and stop the mail when I call the school to tell them you won't be there tomorrow. Get moving. As soon as I pack us up and make a thermos of iced tea, we're leaving. We're going to California!"

Still in shock, I asked her, "Does Daddy know we're coming?"

"Of course not," Mama replied. "He didn't get to vote because he left yesterday and missed the meeting. We'll call him on the way. You two girls help Scooter pack a bag."

We locked up our house, threw our backpacks and a suitcase for Mama in the trunk, and piled into the car. We were headed west again. I couldn't help but wonder what my classmates would think tomorrow at school when I didn't show up and the teacher told them we were gone. Normal people don't just up and go to California on a whim.

When we reached the Texas border, Mama stopped at the first filling station that had a pay phone, and used it to call Daddy with our big news. She even held the phone out so Pat and I could hear.

"I called a family meeting and we all voted," my mother told him before he could say a thing. "The vote was unanimous. The four of us are moving to California."

"You're doing what? You voted on what?" he shouted.

"We're all four in the car and heading west to join you," she said. "We had a family meeting and we all voted. We're on our way to California. The house is locked up, and we just crossed the Oklahoma border into the Texas panhandle."

There was a long silence, and then my father said, "All I can say is thank God the four of you have more sense than I do. The minute I left, I knew I'd made the wrong decision. It seemed reasonable for the girls to stay in school in Pryor, but I don't know what I was thinking. We've all been away from each other far too long. I can't wait 'til you and the kids get here." The phone went silent for just a second, and then we heard: "Nope, I'm not waiting. I'll have one of the guys fly me to Amarillo. I can be there in a couple of hours. Meet me at the airport, and I'll drive the rest of the way to California with you."

We picked up my father at the Amarillo airport and became a family again. Okies headed west once more. No more separations. We were on our way home, wherever that was. Permanent doesn't have that much going for it anyway.

The only permanent thing I need is my family.

And wherever all of us are, well, that's home.

My daddy came home.

Author's Note

My husband was thirty-nine years old when he left Vietnam and came home. He gave Pat and Becky away at their weddings in his dress blues—I made sure they were dry cleaned. He saw his son Scott become a Marine, complete with his father's ivory-hilted sword.

Five years after Ken retired, we had another son, Jon, who never knew what the war in Vietnam was about. Thank God.

I'm grateful my husband and my children's father lived through that terrible time. So many did not. I grieve for all those children whose fathers didn't return from Vietnam. I grieve for the children of all the fathers and mothers who have been lost in war.

For a long time, I would remember and relive all the anxiety, all the difficulties of Ken leaving for the war in Vietnam. Only after many years did I realize what the children had gone through. I had simply been trying to hold the family together for the thirteen months he was gone. Trying to keep our lives somewhat normal and protect my children from worry, pain, and fear as much as was possible. I failed.

Through the years, as they began to share their memories, I heard their hearts and began to write the story of what my children went through during that war, a war in which more than 58,200 Americans died. It is also the story of every child who lived through that war and was afraid—and who had no voice.

The process of telling this story was so difficult to recall and relive that it took me more than twenty years to finish.

As for the personalities in this book, they are somewhat fabrications, a mixture of each of us. Except for Scott. You can't fabricate Scott.

The events and emotions are real.

Ken lived to be eighty-four and is buried at Arlington. Next to Amy. Directly across the street from the Tomb of the Unknown Soldier.

Acknowledgments

I am indebted to my friend Carolyn Brown who spent multiple hours correcting, encouraging, and helping me rewrite. I could not have done this book without her and my oldest daughter, Pat, who spent many hours helping me as well.

I also want to thank my editor, Jeanne Devlin, who spent countless hours explaining methodology and the intricacies involved in publishing my first book.

This book was written for my children and every other child who sent a parent to the Vietnam war and spent months, sometimes years, waiting to see if they would come home.

It is also written for the children whose parents died serving our country as well as those whose hearts were broken when their parent became a prisoner of war or never returned.

I want to further acknowledge all the children since Vietnam who have watched their parent walk out the front door to leave them and go and serve our country. God bless the children.

About the Author

Janie Jacks is a former military wife and a mother. As a U.S. Marine, her late husband, Ken, flew one hundred missions in Korea and another hundred in Vietnam. Janie writes the blog *Janie's Cup of Tea*, and makes her home in central Oklahoma. *The Letter* is her first book.